THE OUTER GAME OF LEADERSHIP

HOW TO UNITE AND INSPIRE TEAMS IN TIMES OF CHALLENGE AND CRISIS

NEURO-RESILIENCE SKILLS
VOLUME 2

PAUL O'NEILL

Copyright © 2025 by Paul O'Neill

All rights reserved.

No part of this book may be reproduced in any form or by any electronic or mechanical means, including information storage and retrieval systems, without written permission from the author, except for the use of brief quotations in a book review.

For Gillian —

a leader whose sparkling strength lies not just in strategy, but in the way she gathers people, steadies them, and lifts them higher.

Your wisdom, joy and indomitable spirit have been both a compass and a quiet inspiration behind every page of this work.

For my mother, Helen O'Neill —

whose faith bore the unbearable, whose laughter lit the dark, and whose love taught me that joy and sorrow walk hand in hand.

You held us together when the world fell apart, keeping a lantern lit when the night was longest. It was that quiet light I followed through my own shadows.

Your spirit lives in every page— and glows softly at the bottom of the spine.

RECOMMENDATIONS

"It's rare that I would use such a word but it's extremely well-earned in Paul's case: he is a visionary. His ability to make the complex simple, to get to the heart of an issue and to recommend an effective solution is outstanding. His vitality and energy is infectious"

Emma Jensen, Head of Go-To-Market, OPTUS

"Through the lens of research in neuroscience, Paul can forge interventions that promote resilience. His type of coaching allowed me to be better equipped to cope with stress and adversity, at my level, but also recognising the signs in other people and helped me being a be manager"

Jessica Scalzo, Variety Improvement Manager at COSTA

"Paul is one of the energizing and gifted leaders I know. He is also one of the most skilled NLP practitioners I have had the good fortune to meet"

Tim Dalmau, CEO at Dalmau Consulting

"As a leader, Paul has a unique quality rarely seen in today's leaders and that is: the ability to find and bring out 'the best' in people"

Tony Enache, CFO at Farm Pride Foods.

"Paul offers a refreshing take on leadership and workplace change strategies. He provides time efficient tailored insights and solutions to support and equip leaders to develop, reframe perspectives and shift the status quo to deliver positive outcomes suited to today's dynamic work environment"

Elizabeth Brockbank, Environmental Manager at ALCOA

"Paul demonstrated a balanced consultative senior management approach that could quickly interpret and translate detailed plans and how they could consolidate into overall strategies for KPI success"

Peter Sheehan, Director GM, Western Sydney Airport.

"Paul is an excellent trainer who has transformed my life. His amazing skills, dedicated care and consistent emotional intelligence has opened a new world for me to view"

Philip Hoang, Data Engineer at CBHS

"Paul has been an invaluable asset to both myself personally and in my business strategies. Paul and his unique skill set have aided constant changes in the business and personal arena that mean I achieved positive rather than negative outcomes personally and financially"

Ben Kavich, Director at Workhorse Group of Companies

"My life was just like 'work-retire-die'. But this has changed dramatically after I had couple of sessions with Paul. With his help, I can recognise myself, again. I learned to love myself and make myself a priority, again. Paul's training has not only changed my life, it changed my whole family's life"

Iris Huangfu, Accountant, Sydney, Australia

CONTENTS

Preface ix

PART ONE
GROUP RESILIENCE SKILLS

Introduction 3
1. THE HIVE MIND 13
2. SAFETY-EMBEDDED STRUCTURES 27
3. SAFETY PRIMING SKILLS 59
Part One Summary 81

PART TWO
MICRO-SKILLS FOR LEADERS

Introduction 93
4. THE ELUSIVE OBVIOUS 97
5. NON-VERBAL ACUITY 103
6. THE SUBTLE SKILLSET 111
Part Two Summary 131

PART THREE
NARRATIVE & UNITY SKILLS

Introduction 137
7. OF SENSE & MEANING 143
8. "BAND OF BROTHERS" 165
9. "LES MISÉRABLES" 185
Key Insights 209

Part Three Summary 211

Conclusion	223
Afterword	249
Notes	253
Bibliography	257
Acknowledgments	259
About the Author	261

PREFACE

Some teams fold in silence. Not all at once—at first, it's just that people stop offering ideas. Then meetings grow quieter. Trust grows thinner. Energy leaks like steam from a cracked valve. Nobody announces the collapse. But you can feel it in the room. In the glance that flicks away too fast. In the joke that lands flat. In the ideas left unsaid.

When that happens, it's already too late for pep talks or performance metrics. The room has stopped listening. The group has slipped into protection mode.

And the leader? Often, they don't even notice until it's over.

This book was written for the leader who *does* notice—who walks into a meeting and senses the tension behind the smiles, the careful silence beneath the talking points. The one who knows something is off but can't quite put their finger on it. The one who's tried clear messaging, feedback loops, team charters—only to watch motivation stall and cohesion fracture anyway.

Because here's the truth: high-performing teams don't just run on goals or plans. They run on trust. And trust, real trust, doesn't live on paper. It lives in the space between people. In the half-second between a challenge and a response. In the look that says, 'You're safe here'—and means it.

This book is not about managing performance. It's about leading signals. It's about reading a room not just by what is said but by what shifts. It's about becoming the kind of leader who can prime safety before a word is spoken—who can guide a team into coherence by presence alone.

You'll learn how to spot the invisible cues—tightened shoulders, hesitant voices, flickers of disconnection—and respond with signals that steady the group rather than escalate the drift. You'll discover practical techniques: how to modulate your tone to de-escalate tension; how to pace a team's state before leading it; how to generate shared direction without forcing consensus. Not gimmicks. Embodied skills. Repeatable. Trainable.

In these pages, you'll meet the concepts of safety-embedded structures and safety priming—not as theory, but as the real levers of group resilience. Because what holds a team together under pressure is not policy—it's culture. And culture is nothing more than repeated signals.

Most leaders wait for team breakdowns before they ask, 'What went wrong?' The leaders this book is written for ask a different question: 'What could we sense earlier, shift faster, or cohere more deliberately?'

So if you've ever led a room where people followed your words but not your energy—where ideas didn't land, trust didn't lift, and alignment felt out of reach—this book will help you see what you missed. And lead what you couldn't yet feel.

Because the outer game of leadership isn't really about control. It's about atmosphere. It's about creating a context so coherent, so steady, that others can step into their best thinking and boldest action without fear.

Much of what this book describes—especially in the early chapters—draws on a lineage that isn't always visible. The suite of techniques used to prime safety owes a quiet but significant debt to the genius of Richard Bandler, whose pioneering work in unconscious patterning and rapid state change opened doors that many of us now walk through instinctively.

And while the PACE structure was developed independently as a coaching compass, it shares a striking genetic resemblance to the maps he drew decades ago. He may not be aware of it—but in spirit, he's the grandfather of this framework.

And when a team starts to move as one, it doesn't feel like you've led them at all. It feels like they led themselves. You simply lit the path they already knew how to follow.

Paul O'Neill

November 2024

PART ONE
GROUP RESILIENCE SKILLS

INTRODUCTION

> *Our biological imperative is to connect with others.
> Humans are not able to flourish without connection.*
> **Dr. Stephen Porges**

The Leadership Imperative

Humans do not thrive in isolation; we think, create, and adapt in groups. From ancient hunting bands to modern corporations, success has never been about individual brilliance but about the intelligence of the collective. Yet, groups can be either extraordinarily adaptive or catastrophically dysfunctional. The factor that determines which path they take is not talent or strategy—it is *psychological safety*.

Without it, groups default to self-protection, stifling creativity and adaptability. Psychological safety is both a goal to be achieved and a fragile condition that must be constantly maintained, shaped by countless micro-signals that dictate what is permissible and what is not.

A leader's role is not to control individuals but to curate the conditions in which people feel safe enough to contribute fully. This requires an understanding that psychological safety is neither static nor self-sustaining. It must be cultivated, protected, and—when necessary—repaired.

The problem for many leaders is that psychological safety is not purely rational. It is not simply about policy or team values; it is embedded in the moment-to-moment signals that people exchange with one another. A dismissive glance, a slight hesitation before someone speaks, a defensive shift in tone—these seemingly trivial cues accumulate into a shared perception of what is permissible and what is not.

This is where most leaders fail—not because they do not value psychological safety, but because they misunderstand how it is created and maintained. It cannot be dictated from above or enforced through a single intervention. It must be embedded into the very structure of group interactions. And this requires a dual approach:

- *Safety-Embedded Structures*: The deliberate, methodical process of creating systems and rituals that align cognition, our intellectual slow-thinking system, to establish shared learnings and understanding. Through these structures, interpersonal trust is built and reinforce over time. This approach is managerial in nature and fosters and supports psychological safety indirectly from the outside-in.
- *Safety Priming:* The visceral, unconscious signals that regulate social interactions in real-time—the verbal and non-verbal cues that shape creates a sense of emotional safety, within each person, which then allows their social engagements behaviours and autonomic invitations to signal safety between people before rational thought even takes place. This approach is flesh-and-blood leadership in nature

and induces psychological safety directly from the inside-out.

To achieve, sustain and repair psychological safety, organisations need both the structured impersonal managerial practices and the fluid interpersonal leadership psychological capabilities. Structured safety ensures that trust is reinforced over time, while instant safety prevents that trust from being lost in critical moments and can repair it rapidly should it be lost.

Psychological safety is not an individual experience—it is a collective phenomenon. A single person may feel confident in their abilities, but if the group as a whole signals caution, hesitation, or defensiveness, even the most courageous will adapt accordingly. Safety is not something individuals bring with them into a room; it is something they find—or fail to find—when they arrive. And that is where the Hive Mind takes over.

Chapter 1: The Hive Mind, we explore how a group of minds is not simply the sum of its parts. It becomes its own entity: a living, emergent system, shaped by unspoken rules, emotional undercurrents and collective behaviour patterns. Before leaders can achieve and sustain psychological safety, they must first recognise that they are not just managing individuals—they are shaping a dynamic network of interdependent minds through *influence*.

Consider a murmuration of starlings. Thousands of birds move as one, shifting direction in breathtaking synchrony. There is no centralised command, no explicit agreement among the birds—only an emergent intelligence that arises as each bird responds to the micro-movements of those closest to it. The result is an adaptive system that reacts to external threats faster than any single bird could on its own.

Like starlings, human groups operate as emergent systems, where individual behaviours are shaped by collective cues. Psychological safety stabilises this system, enabling adaptive intelligence rather than defensive paralysis. These are patterns of connection and protection, often elusive and unseen, but at the group level.

We take our cues from those around us, often unconsciously through our neuroception. Who speaks and who remains silent? Which opinions gain traction, and which are ignored? These patterns are not determined solely by logic or expertise but by a complex interplay of mimicry, emotional contagion and social signalling.

A team does not need explicit rules to suppress dissent—witnessing the subtle punishment of those who challenge authority is enough. Once a negative dynamic sets in, a team's intelligence collapses into defensiveness, and the Hive Mind turns from a connective pattern of adaptive intelligence into patterns of protection for oneself and one's clique.

This is why psychological safety is not just an individual experience but a property of the group itself. A single person may be courageous, but if the Hive Mind leans towards caution and self-preservation, their courage will be constrained by the surrounding atmosphere. In the face of this context, neuro-resilience training enables people to sustain a robust sense of safety.

However, for most people, their safety sense not robust. Indeed, even if explicit danger and threat cues are not detected, an absence of safety cues will often trigger an averse neuroception. *Nothingness is somethingness* when it comes to our evolved neurology; because those predecessors whose bodies assumed safety, and not danger, were removed from the gene pool.

When the Hive Mind is functional, it enables adaptive intelligence—a state in which the group remains flexible, able to integrate new ideas, and unafraid of complexity. When dysfunctional, it collapses into rigidity, conformity, and defensive self-preservation.

Leaders who fail to recognise this focus too much on individual performance and too little on the system in which that performance occurs. They assume low engagement is a motivation problem rather than an environmental one. They misdiagnose symptoms as causes.

The solution is not to order people to "speak up" or "be more engaged" or "have fun". The solution is to change the terrain, not the traveller—to create the conditions within which people feel safe enough to contribute fully. This requires structured interventions that ensure the Hive Mind does not drift into dysfunction but remains aligned, adaptable, and psychologically secure.

Because, while psychological safety feels natural when it is present, it does not emerge naturally: the 'nothingness is somethingness'[1] phenomenon will suppress it. It must be elicited and repaired by sufficient cues of safety, both neurologically systemically.

In Chapter 2: Safety-Embedded Structures, we consider psychological safety and what kinds of management structures can help. Consider a scenario familiar to anyone who has worked in a team. A high-stakes meeting is underway. The issue at hand is complex, requiring decisions that will have lasting consequences. Around the table sit capable, intelligent professionals—each with something valuable to contribute. And yet, the discussion is oddly muted.

Some people speak, but cautiously. Others remain silent, even when their expertise is directly relevant. Those who do contribute hedge their statements, wrapping their points in careful qualifications: *"I might be wrong, but..."*, or *"Just playing devil's advocate here..."*. No one outright disagrees, but nor does anyone push bold, creative, or unconventional ideas.

What has gone wrong? The leader of this meeting might assume the team lacks confidence or engagement. But the issue is rarely about motivation. More often, it is about psychological safety—or the absence of it.

Psychological safety does not mean agreeableness or harmoniousness; it means *the presence of interpersonal safety*. In an unsafe environment, people do not openly disagree, challenge, or propose risky ideas —not because they lack opinions, but because the cost of speaking up feels too high. The issue is not competence; it is an unspoken social calculus, made in real time, about what is socially and professionally permissible.

Leaders must understand the limits of management practices that foster and encourage psychological safety. It cannot be expected or requested any more than it can be imposed within a group. It is something nonlinear in its nature and what works for one team might not be sufficient for another team. However, it can be enabled and made more likely through reliable, repeatable processes that support alignment and group function.

One of the greatest but least visible threats to team effectiveness is *cognitive misalignment*—subtle, unspoken differences in how individuals interpret expectations, priorities, and boundaries. People assume they are working from the same shared understanding, but these assumptions often diverge in ways that remain invisible until conflict arises.

One person believes candour is valued; another believes hierarchy dictates truth. One assumes mistakes will be treated as learning opportunities; another fears failure will be remembered long after it is corrected. These misalignments, if left unaddressed, create fault lines in trust and cohesion.

Structured safety ensures that misalignment is surfaced and corrected before it hardens into disengagement. Knowing 'the rules of the game' creates predictability, making it clear to team members what is expected, what is encouraged, and what will be met with resistance. This structured approach ensures that psychological safety is not left to personal confidence but is embedded into the way the group thinks and functions.

One of the most effective ways to do this is through *structured group reflection*. *After-Action Reviews* (AARs) depersonalise failure, turning mistakes into shared learning opportunities. Similarly, *Crumple & Toss* allows teams to surface tensions anonymously, fostering open dialogue without individual risk.

Also, strength-based analysis techniques—such as *Gold Seam Mining*—shift attention away from risk aversion and towards reinforcing competence. When people see their contributions recognised and valued, they feel *less need for self-protection and more willingness to engage*.

Structured safety is effective because it *removes ambiguity*. In the absence of clarity, people default to defensive strategies—withholding ideas, softening language, filtering out potential risks before they are even spoken aloud. Structured interventions counteract this tendency by making expectations explicit, predictable, and repeatable.

But structured safety, for all its necessity, has a big limitation: it takes time. It is a gradual process, working through deliberate reasoning, repeated interaction, and ongoing reinforcement. It is an excellent long-term regulator of trust, but it does not account for the real-time nature of human interaction.

There are moments—high-pressure meetings, unexpected conflicts, interpersonal tensions, external shocks—where trust is not built but tested. In these moments, people do not stop to assess whether they feel psychologically safe. They react instinctively, based on immediate cues. If those cues suggest threat, no amount of structured safety will prevent the group from slipping into defensive behaviours.

This is why leaders must also learn *safety priming*—the ability to regulate trust at a neurological level, in real time.

In Chapter 3: Safety Priming Skills, we delve in to how leaders can generate psychological safety rapidly. Trust is often spoken about as something that develops gradually—through repeated positive interactions, shared experience, and reinforcement over time. While this is true, it is only half the story. Trust is something we feel instinctively and emotionally before we understand it cognitively.

See yourself walking into a room where two people have just had an argument. No one tells you what happened. No words are exchanged. And yet, you *feel* it—an unease in the air, a stiffness in posture, a subtle but unmistakable shift in the way people hold themselves. This is not intuition; it is neuroception, our unconscious assessment of whether an environment is safe or threatening. And here is the key insight:

The body tells the brain whether it is safe, not the other way around.

This is why safety priming operates *from the inside out*. While structured safety reinforces trust over time, safety priming is *rapid co-regulation*, preventing small ruptures from escalating into defensive postures and disengagement.

The best leaders do not rely solely on structured processes to maintain trust; they *regulate it in real time*, through subtle but powerful non-verbal and verbal cues that shape group behaviour before anyone consciously processes what is happening.

One of the most powerful mechanisms for instant safety is *vocal prosody*—the modulation of tone, rhythm, and cadence in speech. People process vocal tone before they process words, and a leader's voice can either escalate stress or regulate it. A slow, warm, steady voice signals reassurance. A clipped, abrupt tone signals urgency, or worse, hostility. This is why tone matters as much as content—not because people are overly sensitive, but because the Reptilian and Mammalian Brains respond to sound before the Primate Brain responds to reason.

Equally important is *non-verbal acuity*—the ability to detect and adjust the micro-signals of interaction before they become problems. A slight narrowing of the eyes, a tightening of the jaw, a sudden stiffness in posture—these are all read instinctively by others, influencing how safe they feel to engage. Leaders who can sense and recalibrate these cues prevent small signals of uncertainty from cascading into group-wide disengagement.

Another critical skill is *pacing and leading*—the ability to match the group's current emotional state before shifting it towards greater openness and trust. If a team is on edge, an overly optimistic leader will seem detached from reality, even disingenuous. But a leader who first acknowledges the tension, mirrors it briefly, and then gently moves the energy towards calmness creates a natural shift that the group follows unconsciously.

And then there is *Co-Regulating Humour*—one of the fastest, most effective ways to break cycles of tension and reinforce social safety. Laughter, used wisely, is not just an expression of amusement; it is a neurological reset, activating the social engagement system and signalling that the environment is non-threatening. A well-placed joke, a moment of shared levity—these are not just mood boosters; they are strategic interventions in group trust regulation.

These techniques work because they bypass the need for conscious reasoning. They clear the pathway for structured safety to function more effectively, ensuring that people do not just *know* they are safe but feel it, instinctively and immediately.

This is why the most effective leaders do not choose between structured and instant safety. They use structured processes to ensure long-term trust formation and instant safety techniques to maintain engagement in the moment.

The leader who understands both does not just create high-functioning teams.

They create teams that stay engaged, adaptive, and resilient—even under pressure.

The Emotional Steward

The real test of leadership is not in moments of stability, where trust is high and collaboration flows easily. It is in moments of uncertainty, disruption, and stress—when pressure mounts, mistakes happen, and tensions rise. Under these conditions, a well-structured organisation absorbs disruption without fracturing. A weakly structured one buckles, psychological safety erodes, and the group shifts from adaptive intelligence to defensive self-preservation—where silence is safer than contribution and interpersonal risk feels too costly.

Resilience is not about avoiding stress but about maintaining cohesion and clarity within it. Psychological safety, when embedded as a self-sustaining system, allows groups to recover, adapt, and grow stronger rather than retreat into fear. But this only happens when safety is engineered into the culture, not reliant on the leader's presence.

The best leaders do not control behaviour; they regulate the conditions for trust and resilience. They ensure that psychological safety is not just an idea but a self-sustaining force *within the group*. When safety is embedded into the groups unconscious presuppositions—when it is no longer dependent on the leader but reinforced by the system itself—teams do not just function. They can become unflappable.

ONE
THE HIVE MIND

The things we fear most in organizations—fluctuations, disturbances, imbalances—are the primary sources of creativity.
Margaret J. Wheatley

THE HIVE MIND, in the natural world, exemplifies the breathtaking coordination and intelligence that can arise from collective effort. Picture a bustling beehive: thousands of individual insects working in perfect harmony to sustain their colony. Each bee, though seemingly insignificant on its own, contributes to a larger system of breathtaking efficiency and adaptability. This synergy is not directed by any central authority but emerges organically, driven by shared goals and instinctual cues. The result is a self-organising system capable of remarkable feats—a living example of collective intelligence in action.

This phenomenon is not limited to bees. We see echoes of the Hive Mind in other species—from ant colonies to flocks of birds that wheel and dive as if guided by a single mind. These natural systems inspire awe because they seem to defy the chaos that often defines human attempts at collaboration. But what if the principles underpinning the Hive Mind could be applied to human organisations? What if we could harness this collective intelligence to create workplaces that are more innovative, adaptable, and resilient?

The concept of the Hive Mind in human organisations is not new. It manifests whenever individuals come together to achieve a shared purpose, whether in a start-up brainstorming session, a surgical team performing a complex operation, or a disaster response unit coordinating under pressure. Yet, the Hive Mind is not without its challenges. While it has the potential to drive creativity and efficiency, it also harbours vulnerabilities. Groupthink, emotional contagion, and resistance to change are just some of the pitfalls that can derail even the most well-intentioned teams.

This essay explores the dual nature of the Hive Mind in organisational settings. On one hand, it is a powerful engine for innovation, capable of synthesising diverse perspectives into groundbreaking solutions. On the other hand, it can spiral into dysfunction when safety and trust are compromised. The key to unlocking the Hive Mind's potential lies in understanding its mechanics and guiding it with thoughtful leadership strategies.

Throughout this exploration, we will draw parallels between natural systems and organisational dynamics, delve into the evolutionary roots of collective behaviour, and examine the role of psychological safety as a foundation for collaboration. We will also introduce narrative framing as a critical leadership tool for steering the Hive Mind, showcasing how effective storytelling can align teams, diffuse tensions, and inspire action.

Consider the story of a major technology company navigating the chaos of rapid growth. Its small, tight-knit team expanded into a sprawling workforce within months, bringing together individuals from vastly different backgrounds and expertise. At first, the Hive

Mind flourished, generating bold ideas and driving exponential growth. But as the organisation scaled, cracks began to appear. Misaligned goals, eroding trust, and poorly managed emotional dynamics led to a breakdown in collaboration. It wasn't until leadership prioritised psychological safety and implemented deliberate strategies to rebuild trust that the team regained its collective strength.

This narrative underscores a crucial point: the Hive Mind is not a static state but a dynamic process. It thrives in environments where individuals feel safe to contribute, challenge, and innovate. It falters when fear, mistrust, or rigidity take hold. The role of the leader, therefore, is not merely to direct but to curate the conditions in which the Hive Mind can flourish.

As we embark on this journey, we will consider the Hive Mind through multiple lenses: biological, psychological, and organisational. We will explore how evolutionary instincts like tribalism and *neuroception* influence group behaviour, and how these instincts can be harnessed rather than hindered. We will examine real-world examples of both triumphs and failures to understand what distinguishes effective collective intelligence from chaotic group dynamics.

Ultimately, this essay is a call to action for leaders. In an era defined by complexity and uncertainty, the ability to cultivate and guide collective intelligence is no longer optional; it is essential. Whether you are managing a team of five or leading a multinational corporation, the principles of the Hive Mind offer valuable insights for building organisations that are not only effective but also resilient and humane.

By the end of this chapter, you will understand the mechanics of collective intelligence, setting you up to employ the frameworks, models, tools, techniques and practical strategies described in the rest of this book. In doing so, we shall unlock the full potential of our *human hives* and shape a future where collaboration becomes our greatest strength.

Human Hives

The term *Hive Mind* often evokes images of insects working in perfect synchrony, but its applicability to human organisations is more nuanced. In its essence, the Hive Mind represents a form of collective intelligence—a system where the whole becomes greater than the sum of its parts. This phenomenon arises when individuals pool their knowledge, skills, and perspectives, creating an emergent property of group problem-solving and decision-making.

To understand the Hive Mind, we must first dissect its components:

1. *Shared Purpose:* In natural hives, survival drives the collective effort. For human organisations, this purpose could range from achieving a business objective to solving global challenges. A shared purpose aligns individual actions, creating a unifying force.
2. *Interdependence:* In a hive, every member contributes uniquely to the whole. Worker bees gather nectar, drones ensure reproduction, and the queen governs the hive's continuity. Similarly, human teams thrive on role clarity and mutual reliance.
3. *Dynamic Communication:* Communication is the lifeblood of any Hive Mind. Bees use pheromones and the "waggle dance" to convey critical information. Humans rely on language, non-verbal cues, and increasingly, digital tools. Effective communication channels are essential for coordinating efforts and avoiding missteps.
4. *Adaptive Behaviour:* The Hive Mind excels in adaptability. When resources dwindle, bees pivot their activities to ensure survival. Human organisations, too, must navigate

change by leveraging collective intelligence to adapt strategies and innovate solutions.

Human organisations mirror the Hive Mind in surprising ways. Consider the technology sector, where agile methodologies emphasise cross-functional teams working collaboratively toward iterative goals. Each "sprint" resembles the dynamic responsiveness of a hive, with members contributing their expertise to achieve incremental progress.

Another example lies in emergency response teams, where shared purpose and clear communication are paramount. These teams operate under immense pressure, often making life-or-death decisions. Their success hinges on the ability to synchronise individual expertise into cohesive action—a hallmark of the Hive Mind.

While the Hive Mind offers immense potential, it is not without its challenges. Its strength lies in its collective nature, but this very characteristic can lead to pitfalls:

- *Groupthink:* When dissent is discouraged, the Hive Mind can devolve into an echo chamber. Divergent perspectives are suppressed, leading to poor decision-making.
- *Emotional Contagion:* Emotions can ripple through a group, amplifying anxiety, anger or fear. This can disrupt rational decision-making and create a volatile atmosphere.
- *Resistance to Change:* The Hive Mind can become rigid, adhering to established norms even when they are no longer effective. This inertia can stifle innovation and adaptability.

These vulnerabilities underscore the importance of skilled leadership. Leaders must create environments where the Hive Mind thrives without succumbing to its darker tendencies. This involves fostering psychological safety, encouraging constructive dissent, and guiding the group toward adaptability.

Technology in the Hive

In today's digital age, technology acts as both an enabler and a disruptor of the Hive Mind. Collaboration tools like Slack, Microsoft Teams, and Zoom facilitate seamless communication, mirroring the intricate signalling systems of natural hives. However, the overreliance on digital platforms can also lead to "digital groupthink", where algorithms and echo chambers reinforce biases.

Artificial intelligence further complicates this terrain. AI systems can amplify collective intelligence by processing vast amounts of data and offering insights. Yet, they also introduce risks, such as the potential for automation to dehumanise decision-making or perpetuate systemic biases.

Case Story: NASA's Apollo Program

The Apollo program exemplifies the human Hive Mind at its best. Faced with the monumental task of landing a man on the moon, NASA brought together thousands of scientists, engineers and administrators. Each played a specific role, contributing their expertise to a larger mission.

Key to the program's success was the alignment of purpose: every individual understood that their work was part of a shared endeavour. Communication channels were robust, with meticulous documentation and real-time collaboration. Most importantly, the leadership fostered an environment where innovation thrived, encouraging team members to challenge assumptions and propose bold solutions.

The result was a historic achievement that showcased the power of collective intelligence. Yet, the Apollo program also highlighted the fragility of the Hive Mind. Internal rivalries, bureaucratic inertia, and the high-pressure environment created moments of tension that required deliberate intervention to resolve.

To SUMMARISE, the Hive Mind in organisations can be defined as:

A self-organising system of collective intelligence, driven by shared purpose, interdependence, dynamic communication, and adaptive behaviour, which enables groups to achieve outcomes beyond individual capabilities.

To be effective, leaders must balance the strengths and vulnerabilities of the Hive Mind, ensuring that its emergent properties align with organisational goals.

The next section will delve into the evolutionary roots of collective behaviour, exploring how instincts like tribalism and neuroception shape the dynamics of the human Hive Mind. These insights will provide a deeper understanding of why we behave as we do in groups —and how leaders can harness these instincts to build stronger, more cohesive teams.

3. Evolutionary Roots of Group Behaviour

Understanding the Hive Mind in human organisations requires a closer look at its evolutionary origins. Throughout history, humans have relied on collective intelligence for survival. From hunting in coordinated groups to building intricate societies, the ability to pool resources, knowledge, and effort has been a defining feature of our species. At its core, the Hive Mind is not a recent innovation but an ancient survival mechanism.

TRIBALISM

Tribalism is one of the most deeply ingrained aspects of human social behaviour. In our evolutionary past, belonging to a tribe increased the chances of survival. Tribes provided safety from predators, a reliable food supply, and support during illness or injury. The need for belonging is so central to human psychology that exclusion or rejection often triggers a primal fear response.

In modern organisations, tribalism manifests in team dynamics, company cultures, and even interdepartmental rivalries. While tribalism can foster loyalty and cohesion, it also has a darker side. The same instincts that bind groups together can create "us versus them" mentalities, leading to silos, resistance to collaboration, and even outright conflict.

Key Characteristics

1. *In-Group Loyalty:* Employees often prioritise the interests of their immediate team or department over the broader organisation. While this loyalty can enhance group cohesion, it may also hinder cross-functional collaboration.
2. *Out-Group Suspicion:* Teams may perceive other groups as competitors or threats. This suspicion can lead to miscommunication, mistrust, and a reluctance to share resources or information.
3. *Cultural Echo Chambers:* Organisational cultures can become echo chambers where dissenting ideas are stifled. While this reinforces the tribe's identity, it limits innovation and adaptability.

The Science of Safety

The concept of *neuroception* sheds light on how humans assess safety and threats within groups. The phenomenon was identified and labelled by Stephen Porges as part of his *Polyvagal Theory*[1]. Neuroception is the brain's subconscious surveillance system which evaluates whether an environment or interaction is safe, dangerous, or life-threatening. This evaluation happens before we are even consciously aware of it.

In organisational contexts, neuroception plays a crucial role in shaping group dynamics. Employees constantly assess their psychological safety—whether they feel valued, respected, and free to express themselves without fear of retribution. When psychological safety is high, the Hive Mind thrives, as individuals feel empowered to contribute ideas and take risks. Conversely, when safety is compromised, employees may retreat into defensive behaviours such as silence, compliance or resistance.

Threat Detection in Organisations

- *Fight*: Open conflict, confrontational behaviour or aggressive responses to criticism.
- *Flight*: Avoidance of responsibilities, withdrawal from discussions or reluctance to engage in decision-making.
- *Shutdown*: Buckling in the face of challenges, inability to take action or excessive reliance on authority figures for guidance.

Leaders play a pivotal role in shaping the neuroceptive landscape of their teams. By fostering an environment of trust, empathy, and transparency, they can mitigate threat responses and create the conditions for collective intelligence to flourish.

Emotional Contagion

Emotional contagion—the tendency for emotions to spread rapidly within groups—is another evolutionary adaptation with profound implications for the Hive Mind. In early human societies, shared emotions helped coordinate group responses to threats. For example, a sense of fear could mobilise a group to flee from danger, while collective joy reinforced social bonds.

In organisations, emotional contagion remains a powerful but often overlooked force. Positive emotions such as enthusiasm and optimism can energise teams, driving creativity and collaboration. However, negative emotions like anxiety, anger or frustration can quickly derail group dynamics, spreading like wildfire and undermining trust.

Managing Emotional Contagion

1. *Model Emotional Regulation:* Leaders set the tone for their teams. By managing their own emotions, they can influence the emotional climate of the group.
2. *Acknowledge and Address Negative Emotions:* Suppressing negative emotions often intensifies them. Instead, leaders should acknowledge challenges openly and provide constructive outlets for addressing concerns.
3. *Foster Positive Rituals:* Regularly celebrating successes, expressing gratitude, and recognising contributions can amplify positive emotions and strengthen the Hive Mind.

Another evolutionary trait that shapes the Hive Mind is *group polarisation*—the tendency for group discussions to lead to more extreme positions than individual members initially held. While this can drive bold decision-making and innovation, it also increases the risk of groupthink and entrenched biases. Contributing factors include:

1. *Reinforcement of Shared Beliefs:* Group members often validate each other's perspectives, amplifying consensus while sidelining dissenting views.
2. *Desire for Social Approval:* Individuals may conform to the group's dominant opinion to avoid conflict or gain acceptance.
3. *Echo Chambers:* Homogeneous groups are more prone to polarisation, as they lack diverse perspectives to challenge assumptions.

Three simple ways to avoid the adverse unintended consequences of group polarisation are:

- *Encourage Diverse Perspectives:* Actively seek out and value differing opinions to counterbalance the tendency toward consensus.
- *Appoint a "Devil's Advocate":* Designate a team member to challenge prevailing ideas, fostering critical thinking.
- *Promote Reflective Dialogue:* Encourage group members to revisit and critically evaluate their decisions before finalising them.

THE HIVE MIND is a powerful but delicate phenomenon. Its success hinges on the interplay between instinctive behaviours and deliberate leadership. While the evolutionary instincts that drive collective behaviour have served humanity well for millennia, their misapplication in modern organisational settings can lead to fragmentation, mistrust, and stagnation. Leaders who fail to recognise these dynamics risk creating silos or reinforcing biases that limit the potential of their teams.

Conversely, leaders who embrace the principles of the Hive Mind—who foster trust, champion adaptability, and prioritise psychological safety—can unlock extraordinary outcomes. These leaders transform instinct into innovation and tribalism into shared identity. They create cultures where individuals are not only aligned in purpose but also feel empowered to challenge, collaborate, and grow.

In environments defined by complexity, uncertainty, ambiguity, and rapid change, the lessons of the Hive Mind are more relevant than ever. Whether guiding a start-up, navigating corporate restructuring, or leading a multinational team, understanding and harnessing collective intelligence is essential. By aligning the mechanics of the Hive Mind with organisational goals, we can build teams that are not only more effective but also more humane. Let us strive to lead with insight, empathy, and resilience, shaping workplaces where collaboration becomes our greatest strength.

The Hive Mind's power lies in its ability to self-organise, adapt, and amplify intelligence. However, this same emergent nature also makes it fragile—left unchecked, it can spiral into groupthink, emotional contagion, or stagnation. The key to harnessing its full potential is not to control it, but to regulate the conditions in which it operates.

This is where formal safety structures and safety priming become essential—working together to _stabilise_ the Hive Mind, ensuring that its collective intelligence remains an asset rather than a liability. Safety embedded structures provide the stability needed for collaboration to be sustained over time, while safety priming ensures that trust and openness are reinforced in every interaction. These elements act as the guardrails that keep the Hive Mind aligned with organisational goals, ensuring that its immense potential is fully realised.

With this in mind, the next chapters explore how leaders can create the conditions necessary for the Hive Mind to thrive—through both structured safety mechanisms and real-time safety priming techniques.

Chapter 2 examines how formal safety structures provide stability but must be actively reinforced through consistent leadership behaviours to sustain and repair psychological safety.

Chapter 3 expands this understanding by exploring how leaders can cultivate emotional and psychological safety through observational acuity, conversational nuance, and behavioural practices—embedding safety into the fabric of daily interactions.

Together, these chapters equip leaders with actionable strategies to not only harness the power of the Hive Mind but also ensure it flourishes under the pressures of modern organisational complexity.

TWO
SAFETY-EMBEDDED STRUCTURES

*The cycle of reciprocity, rupture, and repair
is the nature of healthy relationships*
Deb Dana

PSYCHOLOGICAL SAFETY IS NOT *JUST* a trendy concept—it's the bedrock of high-performing, resilient teams. It is the felt sense of safety in expressing oneself without fear of adverse consequences. This directly impacts team dynamics, innovation, and performance in measurable ways.

Humans are inherently social, wired for group welfare. Psychological safety taps into this instinct, providing teams with the stability they need to excel. In this chapter, we'll explore what it is, how to cultivate it, and how to sustain it over time. Drawing on the ideas of primal instincts and emotional regulation, we'll outline a framework for leaders to create environments where people feel secure, supported, and free to contribute.

Psychological safety cannot be mandated—it must emerge from the right conditions. Formal structures help by reducing ambiguity, aligning expectations, and ensuring that failure, risk-taking, and dissent aren't punished. But structure alone isn't enough. A leader may implement check-ins and reviews, yet if vulnerability is met with punishment, safety dissolves.

This is the paradox of formalised safety: it can create conditions for trust but cannot guarantee it. Psychological safety is not a compliance exercise—it is built through real interactions. Ultimately, leadership behaviour determines whether a safety structure fosters trust or merely exists on paper.

PERSONAL PSYCHOLOGICAL SAFETY

There's a certain *lightness* in those who feel psychologically safe—a quiet confidence that allows them to *show up fully*, unguarded, without rehearsing every word before they speak. It's the freedom to admit a mistake without fearing a career-limiting consequence, to ask a question without bracing for a condescending response. It's the *absence of that internal, grinding hesitation*—the one that makes people second-guess whether to contribute, whether to disagree, whether to take the risk of being *seen*.

The best way to spot psychological safety in action? It's not just about the ease of speaking up—it's about the *willingness to listen*. Those who feel safe don't need to dominate conversations or protect their ideas at all costs. They stay open, *curious*, even when faced with contradiction. They don't collapse into defensiveness, because they trust that disagreement isn't an attack—it's an opportunity.

And that's where safety breeds innovation. When people feel secure enough to experiment, to take small intellectual risks, they begin *testing the edges* of what's possible. Mistakes become teachers rather than threats. Creativity flourishes, not because risk disappears, but because the *fear of retribution does.*

GROUP PSYCHOLOGICAL SAFETY

A truly safe group isn't just one where people *avoid conflict*—it's one where they *engage fully*, knowing that their voices matter. It's not just the absence of hostility but the *presence of something deeper*—a collective willingness to think together, challenge ideas without undermining trust, and *lean into discomfort* rather than retreat from it.

In a group with high psychological safety, ideas don't just bounce around—they *ignite*. Conversations flow with an energy that isn't about competing for dominance but about *co-creating something better*. Even disagreements take on a different tone—there's curiosity rather than contention, a search for understanding rather than a battle for position. The quietest person in the room feels just as entitled to speak as the most senior leader.

But the *real test* of psychological safety? How the group treats *mistakes*. In a fragile culture, errors trigger blame, shame, or silence. But in a *resilient* group, mistakes become stepping stones—an invitation to learn, to adapt, to improve. Risk-taking is no longer an individual burden but a *shared endeavour*—people dare to put forward bold, unpolished ideas because they trust the group to engage thoughtfully rather than dismissively.

At its core, group psychological safety is about *more than speaking up*—*it's about being heard*. And when that happens, collaboration shifts from being a process to being *a force*—one that makes teams not just *functional*, but *formidable*.

Building Blocks

Psychological safety isn't something you can *mandate*—it's something that *emerges*. You can install all the right structures—open-door policies, anonymous feedback systems, regular check-ins—but if the underlying culture contradicts them, they become *empty gestures*. A team won't speak freely just because there's a process for it; they'll speak freely because they *trust* that doing so is genuinely welcomed, not subtly punished.

Trust isn't built through policies—it's built through *patterns of behaviour*. A leader who *asks for input* but reacts defensively when challenged creates a contradiction that no framework can fix. If people sense that honesty comes with risk, they'll *default to silence*, regardless of how many times they're told to "bring their whole selves to work."

At the heart of this is neuroception—our unconscious ability to detect safety or threat. People don't just *listen* to what a leader says; they *read* their posture, their tone, their micro-expressions. Psychological safety depends on both Inner Game (autoregulation) and Outer Game (co-regulation). A leader who masters their *Inner Game* can project genuine confidence and calm, creating stability for the team.

Take Jill. She *wants* open dialogue and tells her team to "speak freely." But her body language—pursed lips, tightened shoulders, subtle frowns—signals discomfort. Her team reads her hesitancy before they hear her words, and instead of an open exchange, the room fills with *cautious calculation*.

Leaders like Jill don't need another policy—they need *awareness*. Without realising it, they're sending out *autonomic warnings*—subtle nervous system cues that say, *danger*. If a leader doesn't know how to manage their own stress, they *radiate instability*, and no one feels safe taking risks in that environment.

This is why *neuro-resilience* matters. Leaders who practice self-regulation techniques don't just benefit themselves; they create a ripple effect of *safety and composure* that stabilises their teams. When a leader holds *their own ground,* they make it safe for others to do the same. And that's when psychological safety becomes *not just a concept, but a reality.*

How Safety is Lost

> "The art of leadership is the ability to bring out the best in others while being willing to grow yourself"
> **Richard Bandler**

Psychological safety is *fragile*—it takes time to build, but it can be shattered in an instant. Leaders don't always erode safety through dramatic failures; more often, it's lost through a series of small, subtle betrayals—inconsistencies, unspoken rules, and contradictions between *what's said* and *what's done.*

Take Davey, a boss I once had. He *believed* in brainstorming, but only if the ideas aligned with *his* thinking. He *invited engagement* but shut it down when it didn't suit him. One moment he'd *micromanage,* the next he'd be *completely absent.* Nobody knew which version of Davey they were getting on any given day, and that killed trust. The official structures said, *We value your input,* but reality said, *Watch your back.*

Psychological safety isn't just about having the right policies—it's about living them. When a leader's behaviour contradicts their words, even well-intended initiatives collapse. And once safety is lost, the cost isn't just silence—it's disengagement, passive resistance, and, ultimately, a weakened organisation. Here are the most common ways safety gets eroded:

1. **Behavioural Inconsistency**

Consistency between a leader's words and actions is crucial for trust. Davey often urged his managers to "pour a bit of treacle down their throats" — his way of saying, be nice to shopfloor workers, keep them motivated, and butter them up for when overtime was needed.

Yet, almost every Friday, he'd check productivity, find something amiss, and order the manager responsible to:

'Kick them to death!'

Unlike the *Red Queen's*, 'Off with their head!', demands in *Alice in Wonderland*, '*Kick them to death*' was Davey-speak for reprimanding someone. One Friday, I questioned the wisdom of the instruction, given that we were going to need the same people to work over time.

Davey's timeless wisdom was, "OK. Once they've been kicked to death, pour some treacle back their throat and get each of the lazy bastards to work four hours overtime".

When overtime turnout was refused by the workforce, he fumed about 'ingrates' and warned, '...there will come a time!..'

2. **Public Criticism**

Public criticism, however subtle, erodes psychological safety. When leaders correct team members in a group setting, it triggers fight, flight, or freeze responses, discouraging risk-taking and collaboration. As discussed in Chapter 5, punishing vulnerability teaches people to hide mistakes rather than learn from them. Even minor public criticism signals that mistakes are unacceptable, stifling growth and creativity.

For example, Davey gathered his senior team for a brainstorming session. Marker in hand, he announced, *"Right—I need some killer ideas to improve shop-floor productivity!"*

My colleague, Sean, offered: *"How about introducing industrially engineered standards attached to an incentive structure?"*

Davey replied, *"We tried something like that fifteen years ago! It was a pain in the arse to administer. Absolutely, fucking hopeless. I'm never going back there".*

Sean said, *"Maybe we could do it better this time".*

Davey rebuked, *"Is there something about 'I'm not going back there' you didn't understand, Sean?"*

After that, there were no other ideas put forward. Davey spent ten minutes rebuking us for a lack of imagination, expressing his disappointment, and saying that he knew it was going to be a waste of time.

3. **Inconsistent Follow-Through**

Leaders who request feedback but fail to act on it signal that input doesn't truly matter, fostering disengagement. To maintain psychological safety, they must follow through—either by taking action or explaining why they can't. Acknowledging input reinforces respect and inclusion.

In true Davey fashion, he impulsively promised a worker, Malky, that the factory would sponsor his son's football team. The donation was small, yet the cost of adding company-logo patches to the jerseys nearly matched it—a fact Davey grumbled about. Weeks passed, and Malky politely reminded him. Davey's enthusiasm had faded, but he stuck to his word. A month later, Malky, now visibly uncomfortable, informed him the patches and donation were overdue and urgently needed.

When the deadline passed, Malky, now desperate, followed up. Davey, in a frosty tone, snapped: *'Look, I didn't think it'd cost this much. Either you or your wife sew the patches, you pay for it, or I deduct it from the donation.'*

Along with a cheque and a bag of patches, Malky left with a bitter, angry expression.

4. **Favouritism**

Fair treatment underpins psychological safety. When leaders show favouritism, others may feel undervalued, discouraging risk-taking and open dialogue. A truly inclusive team culture requires consistent recognition of all contributions.

Davey's favourite was Sally—"Sal" for short—his finance manager and numerical lifesaver. She was his secret superpower, his crutch. In his eyes, she could do no wrong.

The numerically inclined shrugged off Sal's special treatment, seeing it as her reward for tolerating Davey. The rest resented her. What began as playful banter morphed into seething frustration.

Davey's jibes, from innuendos about *'spreadsheets and bedsheets'* to quips like:

- *"Are you working that sum out with a crayon or just colouring it in?"*
- "Learn to count like Sal and you'll get out early on Fridays too."

Whilst Davey's mockery might have begun as jovial banter. But what is banter when psychological safety is in place creates seething resentment, as well as other patterns of protection, when it is lost.

Leaders rarely set out to erode psychological safety, yet the pressures of high-stakes environments can drive subtle but corrosive behaviours. These missteps, though often unintentional, accumulate quickly, fraying trust, stifling open dialogue, and dulling a team's collective intelligence. Awareness is the first defence. A leader who understands the fragile architecture of safety is better equipped to protect it.

The sections ahead offer practical strategies to reinforce a culture of trust and resilience. Encouraging productive failure through After-Action Reviews helps normalise learning from mistakes. A strengths-based approach like *Gold Seam Mining* shifts focus towards what is working, fostering motivation and engagement. For teams where safety has been fractured, *Crumple & Toss* offers a structured way to restore open dialogue.

Psychological safety is neither an abstract ideal nor a passive state—it is an ongoing practice. Leaders who commit to sustaining it unlock higher levels of creativity, adaptability, and collaboration. The effort is continuous, but the payoff—a culture where individuals feel secure, valued, and empowered—is well worth it.

Strategies for Safety

Having formal safety structures in place is a necessary starting point, but it is not enough. For these systems to be truly effective, they must be reinforced through leadership behaviour that is predictable, consistent, and emotionally attuned to the team's needs.

The following strategies are designed to bridge the gap between formal safety structures and the real-time leadership actions that make them meaningful. By embedding these approaches into everyday leadership practice, psychological safety becomes not just a structural expectation but a lived experience within the team.

Having recognised the importance of psychological safety and the common pitfalls that can undermine it, we now turn to practical strategies leaders can employ to build and sustain this essential aspect of team culture. The following approaches offer structured, actionable methods to foster a psychologically safe environment where individuals feel empowered to take risks, contribute ideas, and work collaboratively without fear.

Productive Failure

In a neuro-resilient environment, failure is a teacher, not a threat. The way leaders respond to setbacks determines whether teams grow from them or retreat into self-protection.

One of the most effective ways to normalise learning from mistakes is the After-Action Review (AAR)—a framework developed by the US Army to enhance performance under uncertainty.

AARs don't analyse failure as an autopsy—they turn mistakes into stepping stones for mastery. The process revolves around three simple but powerful questions:

1. **What really happened?**

The first question helps teams build a shared understanding by integrating diverse perspectives, creating a fuller picture of events. Research by Varela and Maturana suggests up to 90% of perception is shaped by personal experiences, assumptions, and beliefs, making this alignment crucial.

2. **What insights did we gain?**

This is where real learning begins. The second question prompts reflection on what worked, what didn't, and why. Leaders should frame it as exploration, not blame, fostering curiosity, critical thinking, and openness to new insights.

3. **How can we improve next time?**

THE THIRD QUESTION shifts from reflection to action, enabling the team to turn insights into practical strategies for improvement.

The AAR is adaptable, ranging from quick 15-minute debriefs to in-depth reflections on complex projects. It supports two learning types: behaviour-based (observing outcomes) and premise-based (examining underlying assumptions).

For example, after a high-pressure project, a team using AAR first establishes a shared narrative, integrating diverse perspectives. They then review successes and challenges without blame, extracting key insights for improvement. Finally, they define actionable steps, enhancing future performance.

By normalising failure as a growth opportunity, AAR fosters psychological safety, enabling resilience, adaptability, and innovation. In a neuro-resilient culture, failure becomes a bridge to progress, not a threat to avoid.

BYPASS SELF-CENSORING

Psychological safety isn't just about permission to speak up—it's about making it easier to do so. In many teams, people censor themselves out of fear of judgment, rejection, or retribution. Even when leaders actively seek input, social dynamics can keep people silent—especially in larger groups where status, power, or past experiences make open discussion risky.

The Crumple & Toss technique is designed to bypass self-censoring by creating a low-risk, high-trust way for teams to surface honest concerns and insights anonymously:

1. Preparation

THE LEADER BEGINS by distributing half-sheets of paper to each participant, asking them to respond to two key prompts:

- *"What concerns or issues are preventing you and the group from progressing?"*
- *"What needs to happen for the group to start moving forward?"*

These questions prompt participants to consider both challenges and solutions, steering discussions toward constructive insights rather than complaints.

2. Crumple & Toss

Once participants have written their responses, they are instructed to crumple the paper into a ball. This symbolic act of crumpling the paper serves multiple purposes: it injects a playful, relaxed element into the process, it signals that there is no need to hold onto these thoughts personally, and it reinforces the anonymity of each contribution.

Participants toss their crumpled papers into the centre or a bucket. After a few exchanges, each picks up a random paper ball, ensuring anonymity and fostering honest contributions.

3. Reading Aloud

Each participant then reads the responses aloud to the group, following a strict rule of no commenting or analysing during the reading. This encourages the team to focus on the content of each response without personalising or critiquing the ideas.

The moment of listening creates a shared experience, allowing team members to hear one another's concerns without the usual filters of ego or fear of judgment.

4. Pattern Recognition

Once all responses have been read, the facilitator gathers the crumpled papers and lays them out for everyone to see. The team is then invited to look for recurring themes or patterns. What concerns are most frequently mentioned? Which issues appear most pressing?

This collective reflection builds a clearer picture of the team's underlying needs, giving everyone a chance to contribute without the pressure of direct ownership.

5. Solution-Focused Discussion

Finally, with the main issues identified, the team is ready to discuss potential solutions. The leaders guide the group through a collaborative discussion, focusing on concrete actions that address the surfaced concerns.

This stage transitions the team from hesitance to action, empowering members to take ownership of the solutions they develop together.

Crumple & Toss fosters psychological safety by enabling anonymous concerns, encouraging honesty, and ensuring issues are acknowledged. This strengthens team trust, belonging, and security.

Surfacing Stories

Stories aren't just words exchanged in meetings; they are the pulse of an organisation. A Hive Mind doesn't store knowledge in static reports—it breathes it in conversations, gestures, and quiet admissions over coffee. Yet, too often, leaders reduce this living intelligence to sterile data points, stripping away the humanity that gives them meaning. A 30% disengagement rate tells you nothing about the quiet engineer whose innovations go unnoticed or the frontline worker whose frustration is masked by polite compliance.

I was once captivated by Dave Snowden's *Anecdote Circles*, a deceptively simple practice that uncovers the raw, unfiltered narratives shaping workplace culture. Organisations don't fail because they lack information—they fail because they overlook the signals hidden in plain sight. The problem isn't missing data, it's missed intelligence.

But translating theory into practice was another story. Managers hesitated, uneasy about surfacing uncomfortable truths. Some found themselves lost in the sprawl of unscripted conversations, struggling to keep discussions on track. Others encountered silent resistance, where teams, wary of power dynamics, withheld the very stories that could spark change.

This is where *PACE Strengths* and *PACE Surfacing* stepped in—not as rigid methods but as subtle, invisible currents guiding the process. Anecdote Circles had the right goal, but the NLP approach embedded in PACE really made them work. Without forcing narratives or imposing rigid template of a structure, PACE creates the conditions for stories to emerge naturally—revealing patterns that no survey or review could ever expose.

PACE Protocol

As I describe in *'The Inner Game of Leadership'*, the PACE Protocol was designed to be both the map and compass for circuitous coaching conversations, allowing me to track where I was in the conversation, and to where I was going next. Even when the dialogue took an unpredictable or meandering path, PACE ensured I had a clear orientation. More crucially, it helped me stay deeply present—fully tuned to the language, tone and body of the client—without getting overwhelmed by the moment's complexity.

The PACE Protocol naturally transitions through four interwoven stages:

- **Permission** – or, put in its long form: 'prime for safety and probe for permission'. Here, the groundwork of trust is laid. Tension is softened, creating an environment where the client feels secure enough to engage. I draw from a range of NLP techniques—observation, conversation, behavioural strategies—as detailed in Chapter 3. Once rapport is strong, I gently test for psychological permission through teasing, humour, provocative questioning, and other subtle methods.
- **Agency** – Clients already possess the capacity for choice; they simply haven't recognised it yet. My role is to reveal that dormant agency, helping them shift from reactive behaviours to deliberate action, reclaiming conscious control over their instinctual responses.
- **Connection** – As emotional regulation strengthens, the client's nervous system moves from defensive to connective modes. A clear indicator? Their sense of humour re-emerges. Lighthearted exchanges signal not just trust in me, but a deeper sense of internal safety.
- **Embedding** – True change must live beyond the session. Through techniques like future pacing, the client rehearses applying their new insights and strategies in realistic scenarios, anchoring these changes into daily life.

Rather than enforcing a rigid sequence, the PACE model offers a fluid structure—providing guidance without suffocating spontaneity. If conversation veers off-course, the framework acts as a subtle navigation tool, not a cage.

What makes this method powerful is its balance: it allows freedom to explore through stories, metaphors, and detours, while still advancing toward meaningful transformation. For leaders and coaches, it provides an adaptable yet dependable strategy to help individuals rediscover resilience and take ownership of their personal evolution.

Why Uncover Tacit Knowledge?

Traditional feedback methods—surveys, performance reviews, post-mortems—promise clarity but often deliver distortion. They take the messy, layered reality of human experience and flatten it into neat, digestible metrics. A 30% disengagement score looks precise, but it tells you nothing about the exhausted project lead who stays silent in meetings, or the ingenious workarounds devised by an overlooked team. Numbers capture outcomes, but they erase context.

The real problem? Feedback is rarely honest. Employees filter their words, dressing up their struggles in neutral, professional language. The higher the stakes, the more politeness replaces truth. And when organisations rely on these sanitised responses, they make decisions based on what people say in safe spaces, not on what's actually happening on the ground.

Most leadership models are reactive, detecting problems only when they've already spread—like diagnosing an illness after it's turned critical. By then, trust is frayed, resistance is entrenched, and valuable time is lost. What's needed isn't more measurement, but early detection—the ability to catch weak signals before they become full-blown failures.

This is where the power of surfaced stories comes in. Unlike imposed analysis, which dissects knowledge like a specimen under glass, stories self-organise. Insights don't need to be extracted—they emerge when the right conditions are set.

PACE Surfacing ensures this happens naturally. The framework is subtle, guiding conversations without stifling them. Participants don't feel like they're being audited or assessed; they feel like they're finally being heard. The result? A steady flow of authentic intelligence—unvarnished, actionable, and infinitely more valuable than any retrospective report.

PACE Strengths[1]

The best conversations aren't forced—they flow. And the most engaged teams don't need to be fixed; they need to be recognised. When I first experimented with an NLP-infused version of Dave Snowden's *Anecdote Circles*, I wasn't looking to solve problems. I was looking to surface what was already working.

It was a volatile time—constant pressure, shifting expectations, and managers exhausted by firefighting. The idea of open storytelling felt risky. What if people focused on grievances? What if tensions rose instead of trust? But that's exactly why I reframed the discussion. Instead of asking teams to expose weaknesses, I invited them to explore their strengths.

It was a simple but powerful shift. People rarely feel defensive about what already works. Unlike traditional retrospectives—where even constructive feedback can feel like a post-mortem—these sessions framed past challenges as stories of resilience, ingenuity, and growth.

And it worked. The impact was immediate:

- Momentum replaced resistance. People leaned in, eager to share insights.
- Defences dropped. Teams felt safe enough to speak freely.
- Morale spiked. Recognising success wasn't just rewarding—it was energising.

The leaders facilitating these conversations didn't have to manage spiralling debates or awkward silences. PACE acted as an invisible guide, structuring the flow without rigid steps. The discussions felt organic, but they were anything but random. Every phase had purpose:

- *Safety Priming*: Sessions opened with recognition and permission-seeking, ensuring psychological safety from the outset.
- *Setting the Frame*: Subtle cues steered teams away from defensiveness. A well-placed phrase—'*Success rarely happens without setbacks*' or '*Rome wasn't built in a day*'— allowed space for past struggles without turning them into failures.
- *Letting Stories Unfold*: Teams revisited their journeys, reliving key moments. Strengths that had gone unnoticed— ingenuity under pressure, seamless collaboration—surfaced naturally.
- *Embedding the Insights*: By the end, what had started as casual reflection crystallised into something greater—shared ownership of success. The conversation wasn't just an exercise; it became an ongoing mindset.

Unlike standard problem-solving tools, PACE Strengths isn't about repairing—it's about amplifying. Small wins compound into unstoppable momentum. Done right, it doesn't feel like a technique. It feels like an effortless conversation.

It's the difference between tossing a pebble into a pond and watching the ripples spread—or digging deep into the earth to mine gold. The first creates waves of engagement within a team; the second extracts and scales excellence across an entire organisation... and that's where *Gold Seam Mining* comes in.

Gold Seam Mining

Great teams don't always realise how good they are. Strengths—real strengths—aren't always obvious from the inside. They feel natural, routine, almost unremarkable. A frontline team develops an instinctive rhythm, solving problems without second-guessing. A department adapts to pressure without needing a blueprint. Excellence, when truly embedded, looks effortless. The tragedy? Most organisations never notice it.

PACE Strengths worked because it kept improvement local, fast, and organic. The insights stayed where they belonged—with the teams who uncovered them. But what happens when you need to scale these strengths beyond a single unit? How do you transform local brilliance into an organisational advantage? That's where *Gold Seam Mining* begins.

Just as miners don't create gold but unearth it, leaders don't impose psychological safety—they reveal and amplify it. The process isn't about fixing problems; it's about finding the gold that's already there and refining it into something lasting.

Scattered to Consolidated Strength

In most companies, high performance is accidental. It happens in pockets—one high-functioning team, an innovative department—but it doesn't spread. Gold Seam Mining changes that. It extracts, refines, and circulates excellence across the organisation.

It's a structured process, but it doesn't feel like one. Done well, it mirrors the natural flow of discovery, ensuring that strengths aren't just recognised—they become repeatable, teachable, and scalable.

Phase 1: *Prospecting*

Most organisations default to scanning for problems, assuming growth comes from fixing what's broken. But real, lasting improvement comes from a different kind of leadership—a shift in attention.

Instead of asking, *"Where are we struggling?"*, high-performing teams instinctively ask:

"What do we already do well, even under pressure?"

The change is subtle but transformative. When people focus on strengths instead of flaws, their thinking expands. Defensiveness fades, curiosity takes over, and suddenly, excellence that was once instinctive but invisible starts revealing itself.

In one session, I watched a team go through this shift in real-time. At first, their responses were cautious—half-joking remarks, a few polite nods. But as the conversation deepened, stories emerged. Someone recalled a moment when everything could have fallen apart but didn't—because of a quick decision made under pressure. Another remembered a time when an unexpected challenge forced them to improvise on the fly, turning a setback into an innovation.

None of these moments had been recorded. No metric had captured them. But here they were—surfacing in conversation, revealing a team's hidden formula for success.

That's how excellence is uncovered—not through structured assessment, but by creating the conditions where people can see, often for the first time, what they've been doing right all along.

. . .

Phase 2: *Excavation*

At first, recognising strengths feels like an observation—*"Oh, that went well."* But the real shift happens when teams begin to break down why something worked.

In one case, a department known for handling high-pressure deadlines with ease had never actually discussed how they did it. When asked what made them so effective, their first instinct was to shrug:

> *"That's just how we work"*

But as the conversation unfolded, patterns emerged. They weren't just good under pressure—they had an unspoken set of behaviours that made last-minute pivots feel effortless. They automatically anticipated roadblocks. They trusted each other's judgment without micromanagement. They had an instinct for simplifying chaos.

For years, this was just "how things worked." But in that moment, the team saw it for what it was: a repeatable advantage that could be scaled and taught to others.

What had once been intuitive and unspoken was now something they could describe, replicate, and strengthen. That's the moment when a strength stops being an accident and starts becoming an asset.

Phase 3: *Refining*

Raw gold is valuable, but only when refined and forged into something lasting. Strengths, too, must be tempered, tested, and deliberately reinforced before they become enduring assets. The same applies to organisational strengths—recognition isn't enough; they must be sharpened into something lasting.

At this stage, the focus shifts from observation to deliberate application. A team might start by recognising that they handle crises well, but the real question is:

"What makes it that way?"

What behaviours make them resilient? What unspoken habits keep them steady under pressure?

For one team, the answer wasn't obvious at first. They assumed they simply had "the right people"—until they started retracing their steps. It wasn't luck; it was a hidden system. They had an instinct for spotting risks early, an unwritten rule of quick check-ins before major decisions, and a culture where asking for help wasn't seen as weakness, but as a shared responsibility.

Once a team recognises not just what works, but why, something fundamental changes. Suddenly, their strengths aren't just talent—they're transferrable knowledge. They can train others, embed these habits into daily work, and scale excellence without losing its essence.

And this is where the *'Look Back & Laugh'* effect kicks in. A moment that once felt like a near disaster becomes a turning point. Teams stop viewing retrospectives as post-mortems and start seeing them as fuel for mastery. The shift is unmistakable: when people laugh at past challenges instead of cringing at them, you know they've turned mistakes into stepping stones rather than scars.

PHASE 4: *Distribution*

Strength isn't an asset unless it spreads. What happens in one high-functioning team should be absorbed by others—not through formal policies, but through shared experience.

Some of the best organisations don't just recognise excellence—they circulate it. It happens informally at first—one team borrows an approach, a leader adapts a method, a new hire absorbs a habit just by watching how things are done.

But when these strengths are actively nurtured—when they become part of how new employees are trained, how teams collaborate, how leaders think—they shift from being isolated successes to organisational muscle memory.

In one case, a team's ability to handle unexpected changes in real time became the foundation for an entire company-wide training initiative. Not because leadership mandated it, but because other teams saw it working—and, like a fire catching in dry grass, they wanted to bring it into their own work.

That's how cultures evolve. Not by enforcing rules, but by making excellence so natural, so embedded, that it becomes second nature to everyone.

Gold Seam Mining vs. PACE Strengths?

PACE Strengths was really designed for small, immediate improvements. It keeps progress within a team, reinforcing trust, engagement, and cohesion on a local scale.

Gold Seam Mining plays a longer game. It takes the best of what works and embeds it across the organisation. Unlike quick wins, this process requires resources, leadership backing, and strategic follow-through.

Think of it like this:

- PACE Strengths is like tossing a pebble into a pond, near where you stand, creating ripples of local engagement.

- Gold Seam Mining is digging deep into the earth, uncovering, standardising and formalising strengths that can fuel an entire organisation.

For me, the momentum started with PACE Strengths, in a very low key, modest way but, as momentum built, the business wanted to take what was their intellectual property and scale it across their organisation. I had really good results from PACE Strengths, which raised my profile and enhanced my career. However, the higher-value, lasting transformations came out of Gold Seam Mining.

When To Use Which?

Scenario	PACE Strengths	Gold Seam Mining
Quick & cheap team management	✓ Best fit – simple and rapid impact	✗ Too complex and resource-intensive
Low budget, decentralised teams	✓ Easy single team implementation	✗ Requires resources and coordination
Organisation-wide initiative	✗ Not designed for scaling	✓ Ideal for codifying and standardising best practices
High Volatility & Defensiveness	✓ Best fit – simple and rapid impact	✗ Requires stability and structure
Continuous local improvement	✓ Teams own process & solutions	✗ Centralised process managed by organisational leads
Formalise & scale excellence	✗ Keeps improvements within the team	✓ Systematically extracts & spreads best practices

PACE *Surfacing*

Insightful leaders don't impose understanding. They create the conditions for it to emerge. Organisations try to bottle intelligence in surveys and reports, but knowledge resists being captured. It moves, shifts, and emerges in hallway conversations, passing remarks, and quiet admissions in moments of trust. By the time leaders see the numbers, the signals have already passed.

I learned this the hard way. After the successful use of PACE Strengths, I saw an opportunity. What if, instead of guiding teams within a defined strength-based frame, we removed the constraints altogether? What if we let stories surface naturally, without forcing structure?

The results were remarkable. When you create the right environment, people tell you exactly what you need to know—without realising they're doing it.

PACE Surfacing achieves this—not through rigid steps, but through imperceptible guidance, ensuring insights emerge instead of being extracted. It feels effortless, but beneath the surface, every phase is carefully designed to unlock deeper intelligence.

1. Setting the Stage for Truth

Truth doesn't emerge in unsafe spaces. Before people share openly, they scan the room for permission—consciously or not. The first few moments of a conversation determine everything. A single hesitant glance, a nervous shift in posture—these are the unspoken cues that tell a leader whether a team is guarded or ready to speak.

I've seen it happen in real time. A simple opening question:

- 'Can you tell me about your experience with this project?'

It isn't just a query; it's a test. The response isn't just words; it's body language, hesitation, the micro-second delay before someone decides whether to speak freely.

This is why the group itself acts as a collective participant. If one person shares candidly, it gives permission for the next. If humour enters the room—genuine, relaxed laughter, not the forced kind—the tension dissolves. It signals that the space is real, not performative.

The goal isn't to control the conversation. It's to build an environment where people naturally drop their guard.

2. Making Honesty Safe Again

Even in well-intentioned discussions, people censor themselves. They frame experiences in ways that sound acceptable, shaping their words to fit the expectations of their audience. The moment storytelling feels like a performance, it stops being useful.

PACE Surfacing shifts this dynamic. Instead of framing stories as explanations, it frames them as contributions—perspectives, not confessions.

A fundamental truth about memory: no one recalls events in a straight line. We reconstruct, we edit, we emphasise details that felt significant at the time. This isn't a flaw—it's the key to unlocking real insights.

So, instead of steering conversations toward "the right answer," a skilled leader guides without force:

- They let silence do the work. The space between words is where real thoughts emerge.
- They resist the urge to correct or clarify. The goal isn't accuracy—it's resonance.
- They encourage reflection, not just reporting. A simple phrase—*"Tell me more about that moment"*—draws out what was nearly left unsaid.

When people stop editing themselves, they start revealing what truly matters.

3. **The Story Beneath the Story**

Most discussions follow a predictable arc. Someone shares a perspective, others nod, a polite exchange follows. But the real insights aren't in what's said first—they're in what follows.

I once watched a routine debrief turn into something far more revealing. A team started discussing a high-stakes project that had almost failed. At first, the conversation stayed on safe ground—the tight deadlines, the external pressures. Then, someone mentioned a moment when everything could have unraveled—but didn't. That was the spark.

Another team member chimed in, remembering how an unspoken trust between them had kept things from collapsing. Someone else recalled how a particular habit—checking in informally every morning—had prevented small issues from turning into crises.

What began as a post-mortem became a revelation. No one had ever formalised these behaviours as "best practices"—yet they were the very things that had saved the project.

This is why conversations must be allowed to unfold naturally. If they had stuck to the agenda, these insights would have remained buried. Instead, they surfaced organically—not through forced analysis, but through the space to reflect, connect, and recognise patterns.

4. **Hearing What Isn't Being Said**

Organisations track what people report—but the real signals are in what people don't say.

A single frustration, voiced once, might be dismissed as an outlier. But when the same tension echoes across multiple teams, it's a fault line forming beneath the surface.

I once sat in a session where people kept making offhand comments—light jokes about a process that "never quite worked," a half-serious remark about a policy "that no one really follows." At first blush, it sounded like casual chatter. But after the fourth or fifth mention, a pattern was clear—this wasn't humour, it was quiet resistance.

Silence isn't proof of harmony. Too often, leaders hold a mistaken belief:

The absence of complaints = The absence of problems.

But the weakest signals are often the most important ones. They show up in repeated jokes, small hesitations, topics that shift quickly before they can be explored. Savvy leaders don't just listen to words—they listen to *patterns*. What's left unsaid often speaks louder than what's voiced: In human interaction and in nature, very often *nothingness is somethingness*.

Why PACE Surfacing Matters

Traditional feedback models fail because they analyse too late and measure too narrowly. They mistake politeness for truth, metrics for meaning, data for intelligence.

PACE Surfacing fills this gap by ensuring:

- Psychological safety enables truth. Fear distorts feedback. Safe spaces encourage honesty, not compliance.
- Real-time awareness prevents resistance. Policies fail when leadership misreads reality. Engaging with frontline stories stops disengagement before it takes hold.
- Adaptive learning becomes continuous. Knowledge isn't static—it evolves daily through shared interactions.

In complex environments, rigid strategies fail. The best leaders don't impose understanding—they cultivate the conditions for it to emerge. This approach equips them to do exactly that—to listen beyond the words, to hear what isn't being said, and to guide strategy with intelligence that truly matters.

SUMMARY

The difference between a high-performing team and a dysfunctional one often comes down to a single invisible factor: *psychological safety*. Without it, creativity withers, mistakes multiply, and disengagement takes root. Like oxygen in a room, its presence is barely noticed, but its absence is suffocating—choking collaboration, stifling risk-taking, and turning workplaces into arenas of silent compliance.

At its core, psychological safety is a paradox: it cannot be imposed, yet it must be deliberately cultivated. Leaders may establish formal structures—regular check-ins, open forums, feedback loops—but these mechanisms are meaningless if vulnerability is punished or dismissed. A system can encourage dialogue, but only consistent, trustworthy behaviour ensures that people actually speak. The moment a leader's body language betrays their words, or engagement is selectively rewarded, safety fractures.

When it's present, safety is felt rather than announced. Individuals display quiet confidence—the ability to speak freely without rehearsing, to ask questions without self-censorship, to treat mistakes as lessons rather than liabilities. Within teams, it translates into a culture where ideas spark, where disagreement fuels progress instead of conflict, and where failure is recognised as an opportunity to refine, not a reason to retreat. The strongest indicator of such an environment is not whether people talk, but how mistakes are handled—are they treated as moments for collective learning, or as ammunition for blame?

Yet safety, no matter how carefully built, is fragile. It takes time to establish but can be shattered in seconds. The fastest way to erode it? Inconsistency. Hypocrisy. Public humiliation. Favouritism. Consider Davey, a leader who preached openness but punished dissent, who championed engagement but wielded fear. His inconsistency poisoned the very structures he put in place, making participation a liability rather than an opportunity.

Or take the silent damage of public criticism. Picture offering an idea in a meeting, only for your manager to shoot it down in front of everyone. Your stomach knots, your pulse spikes, and suddenly, silence feels safer than risk-taking. This is how safety is lost—not through grand betrayals, but through small, repeated moments of learned helplessness. Just as damaging is the failure to follow through—when leaders invite feedback but fail to act, they teach people that contributions are performative rather than meaningful. Favouritism compounds the problem, dividing teams into insiders and outsiders, breeding quiet resentment where trust should be.

Restoring lost safety requires more than platitudes. It must be embedded in practice. After-Action Reviews (AARs) reframe failure as an opportunity for collective learning, ensuring that reflection leads to improvement rather than blame. The Crumple & Toss technique creates a structured space where honesty can thrive without fear of reprisal, allowing the unsaid to surface.

But safety isn't just about preventing harm—it's about amplifying strengths. Inspired by Dave Snowden's narrative methods, PACE Surfacing helps leaders uncover the hidden intelligence within teams. While organisations focus on data, they often overlook the tacit knowledge embedded in daily interactions. Stories—shared or withheld—reveal the true culture of an organisation. Leaders who create the right conditions for these stories to emerge don't just receive insights—they gain an unfiltered window into reality.

Successful executives don't just protect trust—they build enduring strength. PACE Strengths and Gold Seam Mining shift the focus from fixing deficiencies to amplifying what already works, creating a culture of excellence rather than mere damage control. Like a skilled miner, a leader must uncover hidden potential, refine insights, and distribute them across the organisation.

Psychological safety is not a static condition but a continuous practice. The best teams don't just survive uncertainty—they thrive in it. The best leaders don't just prevent harm; they create cultures where people dare to think, speak, and build something greater than themselves.

THREE
SAFETY PRIMING SKILLS

> When people learn to laugh at what used to terrify them, they are free[1]
> **Richard Bandler**

THE SAFETY SENSE is a necessary but not sufficient condition for *permission*. That's why, in the PACE Protocol, safety priming is the first priority—engaging observation, conversation, and behavioural aspects from the very first interaction.

Just like driving through a busy town centre, leadership requires constant awareness and real-time adjustments. Every interaction, every response, and every non-verbal cue determines whether the environment feels safe or uncertain. This chapter is about applying your inner and outer game skillsets to safety priming, equipping you with the tools to create, sustain, and repair psychological safety in real-time.

These techniques range from foundational skills—such as breath control and observational acuity—to more nuanced conversational and behavioural strategies. As you gain fluency, you will learn to experiment and refine these approaches, much like an artist blending colours to create a masterpiece.

While safety priming is an active, dynamic process, it does not replace formal safety structures. Formal safety provides *predictability and stability,* but only safety priming can create *immediate, real-time trust*—activating safety embedded structures and making them meaningful in practice. Without skilled safety priming, even safety embedded structures risk becoming hollow—policies exist, but psychological safety remains absent. The techniques in this chapter bridge that gap, ensuring that safety is not just an institutional goal but a lived experience within the team.

STAGE 1: Observation

A leader's ability to prime safety begins with keen observation. In NLP, we refer to this as 'sensory acuity'. Like a ship's captain steering his vessel through changing waters, the leader who reads subtle verbal and non-verbal cues is prepared to adjust their approach.

Observational skills help you assess your team's current state, revealing when they're relaxed, tense, or in need of reassurance. Here, we introduce key observational techniques that empower you to sense and respond to the emotional undercurrents that impact team performance.

To attain heightened sensory acuity, you need to be in a grounded, alert state, where you focus is entirely externally oriented. For me, to support myself to be fully concentrated on what is going on around me, I fire an 'anchor' which turn on

- A state of fascination
- Keen awareness of my peripheral vision.

Once these aspects are in play, my senses are alert, and I am *in the moment*.

Breathing Patterns

Breathing is more than a simple bodily function; it's a window into a person's emotional state. High, shallow breaths in the chest often signal stress or anxiety, while low, deep breaths in the abdomen indicate relaxation and control. As a leader, observing these breathing patterns in both you and your team can serve as an early indicator of emotional readiness. If you notice shallow, rapid breathing during a meeting, for instance, it may suggest heightened tension or unease—a cue that safety priming techniques could be beneficial.

Exercise: Practice observing your own breath before important interactions. Take a moment to lower your breathing to your abdomen, bringing calm to your body.

As you interact with your team, observe their breathing, particularly during high-stress discussions, to gauge when a grounding exercise might be helpful.

Also, see if you are able to identify a baseline for each of them: some people naturally breathe higher or lower. Calibrating this is useful because it's the change in their breathing pattern that is the meaningful cue.

Physical & Emotional Cues

Our bodies communicate continuously, often revealing emotions we may not verbalise. Recognising cues such as stiffness in shoulders, clenched fists, fidgeting and fleeting expressions of tension or discomfort can help you detect the team's underlying feelings.

Facial expressions, posture, and vocal tone often change subtly in response to anxiety or comfort, giving you insight into whether your team feels psychologically safe or if they're operating under pressure.

As with breathing, it's useful to calibrate a baseline for person – for example, when someone who fidgets a lot become still, that's what's important. Also calibrate a baseline for the group: being alert and noticing when baseline noise and activity levels shift is important.

> ***Pro Tip***: Try noting body language patterns during a routine team meeting. Do you notice any changes as specific topics are discussed? A team member sitting back with arms crossed might suggest disengagement or defensiveness, while relaxed, open postures signal comfort and trust. Recognising these cues allows you to adjust your approach, promoting a more open and connected environment.

Group Dynamics

In both coaching and team settings, the level of the group's cooperative accord, it's unity and cohesion, although distinct from, it is indicative of the group's safety level. Observing how team members respond to playful or probing comments can help you assess whether safety is strong or needs reinforcement. If your light-hearted question or comment is met with smiles and engagement, safety is likely intact; if team members appear uncomfortable or closed off, it may be time to refocus on priming safety.

> **Exercise**: At your next team meeting, begin with a light-hearted question or brief personal story to gauge initial rapport.

Observe reactions—smiles, laughter, or relaxed postures typically indicate strong rapport, while tension or silence may suggest areas for growth.

Building rapport creates a foundation for safety priming, encouraging team members to engage more openly.

Co-Regulation

Co-regulation is the act of using shared neurological and emotional states to restore and maintain connection within the team. A leader who remains grounded in moments of stress can actively regulate the team's collective emotional state, reinforcing stability even under pressure.

The mechanism by which this occurs is subtle but powerful: the leader's composure sets the baseline for the group's *neuroception*, allowing team members to mirror and absorb their emotional steadiness.

As you practice safety priming techniques, observe how others' demeanours shift in response to your grounded, centred behaviour. Co-regulation allows your team to *unconsciously synchronise with your emotional state,* which can reduce collective tension and enhance receptivity to guidance.

> ***Pro Tip***: Next time you enter a high-stress meeting, focus on regulating your own emotions. Take a few deep breaths and maintain a relaxed posture. Observe whether others in the room also begin to relax, signalling that co-regulation is taking effect. This shared calmness can be a powerful tool,

helping teams remain focused and connected even in challenging situations.

Safety priming is only as effective as its consistency. Leaders who apply these techniques sporadically—exuding warmth one day but reacting defensively the next—create uncertainty rather than trust. Because the nervous system continuously scans for safety or threat, inconsistent leadership behaviour triggers hypervigilance, making team members hesitant to engage. Trust is built through predictability.

The most effective safety primers are not just skilled communicators; they are dependable ones. Every interaction, every non-verbal cue, and every moment of engagement must send a clear, aligned message:

'This is a space where you are safe to contribute'

Stage 2: Conversation

If the Hive Mind is the system through which psychological safety is shaped, then safety priming is the mechanism through which leaders regulate it in real time. Safety cannot be demanded, nor can it be enforced through policy alone. It must be cultivated at a physiological and social level, through every interaction, micro-cue, and exchange of trust.

The most immediate and continuous form of safety priming is conversation. A leader's voice—its tone, rhythm, and cadence—can either steady the nervous system or trigger defensiveness. Their choice of words can either invite participation or stifle engagement. Safety priming operates within this emergent system, using verbal and non-verbal signals to reinforce trust as rapidly as the group perceives safety or threat—before rational thought has even taken place.

Formalised safety structures provide stability and predictability over time, but they cannot, on their own, elicit psychological safety. Conversational skills are the real-time *stabilisers* that determine whether those structures feel meaningful or performative. A team may have policies that support trust, but without reinforcing interactions, those policies remain theoretical rather than lived experiences.

In leadership, how you speak matters as much as what you say. Conversational skills in safety priming rely on tone, humour, empathy, and clarity to create an environment where team members feel comfortable expressing themselves. Mastering these skills involves both content and delivery—each exchange, even the briefest comment, can either strengthen or undermine psychological safety.

The following conversational techniques will equip you to foster trust, reduce defensiveness, and guide your team toward open, constructive dialogue.

Vocal Prosody

The voice has a profound influence on how people feel and react. When leaders adopt a calm, melodic, and rhythmic tone, they can ease anxiety, encourage trust, and promote a sense of security. Vocal prosody, or the modulation of pitch, tone, and rhythm, can subtly signal that everything is under control, helping to calm team members during stressful situations. Think of how a lullaby soothes a baby; similarly, a well-modulated voice can help your team relax and feel safe to contribute.

> **Exercise**: Practice vocal modulation by recording yourself speaking about a challenging topic, focusing on maintaining a calm, downward-sloping vocal pattern. As you listen back, ask yourself whether your tone conveys reassurance and stability.

Over time, this practice will help you naturally set a calm tone in real-time, especially useful in high-stakes or tense meetings.

Playfulness & Humour

Humour and playfulness are powerful tools in safety priming, helping to break down formal barriers and make people feel at ease. Playfulness triggers the brain's social engagement system, which reduces defensiveness and invites connection. By opening with a light-hearted question or sharing a funny, relatable anecdote, leaders can foster an atmosphere of openness and camaraderie. Playfulness also signals that it's safe to let one's guard down—a vital component in building safety.

> **Example**: Start your next team meeting with an unexpected, light-hearted question, like "If you were a superhero, what would your power be?" or "If your workday was a movie genre, which one would it be today?" This simple act shifts the team's focus from task-oriented tension to something lighter, encouraging everyone to laugh and relax.

> ***Pro Tip***: Notice the reactions. If people laugh or respond playfully, the team is likely in a good

place rapport-wise. If they're hesitant, more work may be needed to build comfort and trust.

Communication Style

In times of change or uncertainty, clear, transparent communication is essential to creating safety. When leaders communicate openly—acknowledging challenges honestly and explaining decisions without defensive posturing—they reduce team anxiety. Verbal empathy, in particular, goes beyond simply proving that you've been listening; it involves validating team members' feelings, showing that their experiences and perspectives have been heard and understood properly. This is received as a cue that they are being respected.

> ***Pro Tip***: When introducing a difficult change, be direct but considerate. For example, instead of saying, "We have to cut the budget," try, "I know this is a challenging adjustment, and many of you may have concerns. Here's how we plan to work through this together." This approach combines honesty with empathy, allowing the team to feel seen, heard, and supported.

Exercise: Practice verbal empathy by restating a team member's concerns in _their own words_. For instance, if someone says:

"I feel like I'm drowning... every time I get a breath; I keep getting dragged under".

Now, *active listening* advocates would have you listen to their words and respond with different words. That would be something like,

"It sounds like you're really struggling"

Certainly, if you were a third party watching the from the outside, such a response is empathetic, as far as it goes. However, if you're the person that feels like you are drowning, that level of understanding doesn't go far enough.

After all, 'really struggling' doesn't have the same degree of visceral intensity as 'near death by drowning', does it? And yet, 'near death by drowning' is how that person is representing their situation both to themselves and to you.

However, if you say, "Drowning... just trying to keep your head above water?", you are engaging with them, and showing that you understand them, in *their* terms... not yours. When you do that, they will feel safer faster and will give you their permission sooner: the primary goal of the "Permission" phase.

Deeper Engagement

Building permission means establishing rapport to a point where team members feel comfortable with more direct, even challenging, conversations. In coaching, rapport is essential for guiding clients through personal insights; similarly, leaders must create an atmosphere where team members feel safe enough to engage with difficult topics. Building permission is a skill that enables leaders to move from superficial interactions to more meaningful discussions that build trust and psychological resilience.

Example: *When you sense a team member is uncomfortable with feedback, start by sharing a positive observation or an empathic comment. As rapport strengthens, introduce constructive feedback gradually, inviting them to share their own thoughts on the matter. For instance:*

"I really appreciate your commitment to the project. I think there's an opportunity to improve efficiency here—what's your view on how we might approach this?"

THIS GIVES them space to engage openly and without defensiveness.

STAGE 3: **Behaviour**

While observational and conversational skills set the foundation, behavioural skills allow leaders to embody safety priming and establish it as part of the team's culture. Behavioural cues, from controlled breathing to relaxed body language, send powerful signals of calm, openness, and readiness to engage. Through consistent use of these behaviours, leaders not only reinforce safety but also invite their team to mirror these states, promoting a collective sense of security and trust. Here, we delve into the essential behavioural skills leaders can develop to create and sustain a culture of safety.

BREATH CONTROL

Regulating one's breath may seem simple, but its effects on self-control and group dynamics are profound. In moments of high tension, slowing down and lowering your breath to your abdomen signals calm and presence, setting a foundation for others to mirror. When a leader models steady, controlled breathing, they signal that there is no need for alarm, which can profoundly influence the group's overall state.

> **Exercise**: Practice "box breathing" before meetings or challenging conversations. Inhale for four counts, hold for four, exhale for four, and hold for four again.
>
> This exercise can help you enter a calm state, which, in turn, stabilises the emotional energy you bring into the room. Over time, you'll notice that your centred breathing has a subtle yet noticeable calming effect on your team, allowing co-regulation to take place.

Playful Engagement

Human connection thrives on direct, face-to-face interaction. Making eye contact, offering a sincere smile, and maintaining a relaxed posture are subtle yet powerful cues that activate the social engagement system.

These small acts establish a baseline of trust and connection, reassuring team members that they are seen, valued, and safe. This is especially critical in times of change or stress when people may feel disconnected or anxious.

> ***Pro Tip***: During team check-ins or feedback sessions, make a point of maintaining eye contact with each participant. Show genuine engagement with each person's input, signalling that their presence matters. This consistent face-to-face engagement will reinforce a culture

where every individual feels acknowledged and valued.

Open Physical Cues

Your posture communicates a great deal about your mindset, and as a leader, adopting a relaxed, open posture can encourage your team to do the same. Avoid crossing your arms or hunching your shoulders—stances that can come across as defensive or closed off.

Instead, aim for a relaxed, upright stance with uncrossed arms and open palms. This openness signals approachability and encourages others to mirror a similar stance, reducing tension and fostering a sense of security.

> ***Pro Tip***: The next time you enter a discussion, pay attention to your posture. Relax your shoulders, uncross your arms, and adopt a balanced stance. Notice how this subtle change impacts the mood of the conversation, helping others feel comfortable and open to contributing their thoughts.

Vocal Co-Regulation

The nervous system's response to auditory cues signalling safety is quite fascinating. The tone, pitch, and rhythm of your voice are integral to setting an emotionally safe environment. Dr. Stephen Porges points to famous American singer Johnny Mathis as an example of prosody.

Younger readers may find 'John Legend' a more relatable reference, with his smooth, warm, and intimate vocals in songs like *"All of Me"*.

Either way, in the context of Porges's work on auditory safety and the calming effects of prosodic voices, he puts it this way:

> "Our nervous system is waiting for Johnny Mathis"

This remark underscores how the modulation of vocalisations in certain sounds (voice, music, etc) can convey safety to our nervous system. In doing so, it promotes relaxation and social engagement: good things for safety priming for groups.

A calm, rhythmic voice can have a powerful co-regulating effect on a group, gently guiding the emotional state. When discussing sensitive topics or leading a tense meeting, adopting a softer, melodic, more 'Johnny Mathis', tone helps others stay centred and engaged. This is especially helpful during high-stakes conversations where anxiety might run high.

> **Exercise**: During your next high-stress discussion, consciously slow down your speech and soften your tone. Observe how this adjustment affects the room's energy and helps bring others into a more receptive, calm state.
>
> Over time, using vocal prosody consistently in tense settings can reinforce an overall culture of safety and trust.

Turn Niggles *into Giggles*

Co-Regulating Humour can be a highly effective safety-priming tool. Gentle coxy humour helps to lighten the mood, reducing anxiety and encouraging people to let go of rigid thought patterns. More robust, well delivered 'chiding' humour, as exemplified by Frank Farrelly and

Richard Bandler, takes more verbal and abductive acuity, but, when mastered, can be the gold standard of priming and probing.

Whatever style adopted, when leaders can turn minor annoyances or "niggles" into playful moments or "giggles", it fosters resilience and an ability to view challenges from a fresh perspective.

This doesn't mean making light of serious issues but rather helping the team keep things in proportion, transforming unnecessary tension into something constructive.

> **Example**: *If a team member voices a minor frustration, such as* "We're always stuck in back-to-back meetings," *respond with a touch of humour, like,* "Maybe we should install bunk beds in the conference room!"
> *This playful reframing encourages the team to laugh and take the frustration less seriously, breaking down any tension and opening the door to solutions.*

> **Pro Tip**: Always gauge the team's response to humour. Playful commentary that is met with smiles and laughter signals a healthy rapport. Take subdued responses as a cue that they need more safety. As such, maintain a state of approachability and jolliness and continue to reframe playfully. In doing so, you are sending lots of safety cues and autonomic invitations to deepen connection.

Daily Safety Priming

Safety priming is most effective when it becomes a daily practice rather than a one-time intervention. Embedding these skills into your regular routines reinforces safety as a constant. This might include starting each meeting with a brief grounding exercise, using humour regularly to diffuse tension, or reminding yourself to check your posture and breathing.

By making these behaviours routine, you reinforce an environment where safety is the norm, not the exception.

Exercise: Create a personal checklist of safety-priming actions that you can refer to before each team interaction. Include reminders such as "take a deep breath," "engage with eye contact and smile" and "use an approachable tone." This checklist will help you internalise these practices until they become second nature, gradually embedding safety priming into your leadership approach.

While safety priming begins at the individual level, its true power lies in its ability to transform entire teams and organisations. A leader can model these techniques, but if psychological safety is to become truly embedded, it must be woven into the organisation's culture.

Scaling safety priming ensures that safety is not dependent on individual leaders but is a shared responsibility reinforced at every level. The next section explores how to embed safety priming into the larger system, ensuring that it is not just a leadership practice but a core element of organisational culture.

Stage 4: Scaling Safety

While safety priming begins with individual interactions, its true power lies in its capacity to transform entire teams and organisations. By embedding safety priming practices into daily routines, training, and leadership development, safety that supports adaptability, resilience, and open collaboration on a larger scale, seeping into the deeper aspects of the organisation's culture.

In this final section, we explore ways to scale safety priming across teams and organisations, transforming it from an individual skill into a foundational cultural element.

Co-Regulation is Wisdom

As individuals begin to mirror the leader's calm and present demeanour, co-regulation emerges as a powerful force within the group. Co-regulation allows everyone to take collective responsibility for the team's emotional state, supporting one another through mutual reassurance and calmness.

When leaders intentionally model and encourage co-regulation, they create a team environment where emotional stability and openness become cultural norms.

> **Example**: *When introducing a high-pressure project or discussing challenging changes, maintain a calm, measured tone and your team members will mirror your calm. In moments of spiked emotion, remind everyone to take a moment to breathe before reacting, that way you are inserting co-regulation into their conscious thoughts.*

Over time, this shared focus on calmness and receptivity will become a natural response to stress, helping the team navigate complexities with resilience.

Feedback Loops

Scaling safety priming requires regular feedback to gauge its impact and identify areas for improvement. Inviting team members to share their experiences with safety priming techniques can offer valuable insights, helping leaders refine their approach and adjust their strategies as needed.

Feedback loops also foster a sense of collective ownership over the team's emotional climate, enabling team members to feel actively engaged in maintaining a safe and supportive environment.

Exercise: Consider implementing regular team surveys or feedback sessions where team members can anonymously share their thoughts on the team's emotional climate.

Ask *PACE Protocol* style questions like,

- *"Do you have the permission to share your ideas, even if contentious, in meetings?"*
- *"When things go wrong, does your group have your back? Does your boss?"*
- *"Are you able to be fully transparent in your group without feeling vulnerable?"*
- *"Think of the future, is your group learning to get better, faster and smarter?"*

This feedback can reveal insights into the effectiveness of safety priming efforts, guiding leaders in refining their practices.

Personal Resilience Training

Embedding autoregulation techniques into leadership development programs ensures that new and existing leaders possess the skills to foster safety. Training sessions can cover core skills like *The Worry Solver, Connect with Yourself,* and *Increasing Instinct Acuity* (see Volume I: The Inner Game of Leadership) equip leaders with practical tools to control their own stress. Additionally, these programs reinforce the expectation that safety is an organisational priority, cascading the impact of autoregulation from leaders to the co-regulation of their respective teams.

> ***Pro Tip***: Design workshops that teach autoregulation skills, such as using breathing techniques to control stress and raises their awareness of their own unique VAK+B patterns.
>
> ***Practical Step:*** Encourage leaders to practice these techniques through role-playing scenarios and real-world simulations. This not only strengthens their confidence in their ability to autoregulate but also embeds these practices within the organisation's leadership framework.

Group Resilience Training

Embedding safety priming techniques into leadership development programs ensures that new and existing leaders possess the skills to foster psychological safety across their teams. Training sessions can cover core skills like observational acuity, vocal prosody, and non-verbal communication, equipping leaders with practical tools to build trust and reduce defensiveness. Additionally, these programs reinforce the expectation that safety is an organisational priority, cascading the impact of safety priming from leaders to their respective teams.

> ***Pro Tip***: Incorporate safety priming training into leadership onboarding and ongoing development programs. Instead of treating it as an individual competency, integrate it into team-wide practices such as structured debriefs, coaching sessions, and collaborative reflection exercises.
>
> **Practical Step**: Train leaders in group-level co-regulation techniques, ensuring they can reinforce safety even in high-pressure environments. Conduct live simulations where teams practice responding to real-time safety ruptures together, reinforcing a collective approach to psychological safety.

Valuing Safety

To fully scale safety priming, psychological safety should be recognised as an organisational value, embedded into core principles and reflected in everyday practices. When safety is explicitly valued, it permeates all levels, shaping how teams approach problem-solving, decision-making, and interpersonal interactions. Reinforcing safety as a cultural value encourages everyone—from frontline employees to executives—to prioritise emotional well-being, making it a unifying aspect of the organisational identity.

> ***Pro Tip***: 'Shift happens', so to speak. Therefore, having experienced coaches on retainer with your organisation, gives you a fast response should safety be ruptured. The speed and effi-

cacy of this approach are truly impressive—as demonstrated with the 'Jerry' case in 'The Inner Game of Leadership'.

External Stakeholders

Safety priming principles can be equally powerful when engaging with external stakeholders, including clients, partners, and the public[2]. By practicing transparency, empathy, and calm presence in high-stakes interactions, leaders can build trust and foster stronger relationships beyond the immediate team.

The same safety cues that promote emotional safety internally can strengthen credibility and collaboration externally, making negotiations, client presentations, and partnerships more productive.

> ***Example***: Consider addressing a board of investors during a challenging financial period. By maintaining a steady, transparent tone and openly acknowledging the difficulties, you create a calm, trustworthy atmosphere. Stakeholders are more likely to remain receptive and cooperative when they feel they are engaging with a leader who is honest, composed, and considerate of their concerns.

> **Exercise**: Before engaging with external stakeholders, take a moment to check your emotional state using breath control or a brief body scan. Focus on presenting yourself with openness and empathy, listening actively and responding thoughtfully. The *'How Not to Get Shot'* technique in Chapter 6, in Part 2, is an excellent way to engage in difficult conversations.

This practice reinforces safety not just within your team but in every relationship your organisation fosters, strengthening your reputation as a trustworthy and emotionally intelligent leader.

Scaling safety priming across teams and organisations transforms it from an individual skill into a cultural pillar. By embedding safety priming in daily practices, leadership training, feedback mechanisms, and organisational values, leaders create an environment where psychological safety is not just a priority—it is an expectation.

When fully integrated, safety priming is no longer a leadership tool—it is the foundation of how people think, interact, and innovate together. In these cultures, trust is not something that must be continually rebuilt; it is the default state. Teams in these environments do not just function—they flourish.

PART ONE SUMMARY

We have a nervous system that reacts to both danger and safety. Social connection triggers a calming response that enhances our ability to feel secure and connected[1]

Dr. Stephen Porges

Part 1, *Group Resilience Skills*, examines the dynamics of collective intelligence within teams and organisations, exploring how leaders can harness the instinctive behaviours of groups to build resilience, trust, and innovation. Grounded in neuroscience, behavioural psychology, and organisational theory, this part reveals how human groups function as interconnected systems, balancing creativity and collaboration with the risks of dysfunction and fragmentation.

Across three chapters—*The Hive Mind, Safety-Embedded Structures* and *Safety Priming Skills*—readers learn how to shape group behaviours that foster cohesion and adaptability.

The Hive Mind is a phenomenon of collective intelligence that emerges when individuals work toward shared goals. Drawing from nature, this chapter illustrates how systems like beehives or bird flocks achieve remarkable coordination without centralised control[2]. In human organisations, the Hive Mind thrives on shared purpose, interdependence, and dynamic communication. However, it is also vulnerable to pitfalls like groupthink, emotional contagion, and resistance to change. The chapter emphasises the leader's role in regulating the Hive Mind, ensuring it serves adaptability rather than self-protection.

Psychological Safety is the foundation of high-performing, resilient teams. This chapter explores how neuroception—our subconscious ability to detect safety or threat—**shapes team dynamics[3]. When psychological safety is high, individuals feel empowered to take risks and contribute openly. When it is absent, they default to defensive behaviours like withdrawal, conflict, or disengagement.

Leaders must cultivate both the Inner Game (self-regulation) and Outer Game (team regulation) to create environments where trust, respect, and open communication are the norm[4]. Structured techniques such as *After-Action Reviews* and strengths-based approaches ensure psychological safety is reinforced over time[5].

Safety Priming builds on structured safety by embedding real-time safety cues into daily interactions. While structured safety ensures long-term stability, safety priming ensures trust is actively reinforced in critical moments. Leaders learn to observe subtle emotional and physical cues, regulate safety using conversational tools like vocal prosody and humour, and model calming behaviours that influence group neuroception.

This chapter also explores how safety priming can scale across organisations, transforming psychological safety from an individual skill into a cultural cornerstone.

PART ONE SUMMARY

Techniques Introduced in This Part

To build and sustain neuro-resilience, we introduced some approaches:

1. **PACE Protocol** – Map and compass for coaching session
2. **After-Action Reviews** – framework for productive operational learning
3. **Crumple & Toss:** Anonymises team member inputs to surface hidden tensions.
4. **PACE Strengths**: Strength-based storytelling for learning and cohesion-building.
5. **PACE Surfacing:** Safe engagement for tacit knowledge and emergent narratives.
6. **Gold Seam Mining:** for uncovering, refining and institutionalising strengths.
7. **Safety-Priming** – batched and sequenced verbal and non-verbal techniques the purpose of accelerated co-regulation.
8. **Breathing Patterns:** Gauge emotional states and regulate team energy.
9. **Co-Regulation** – Making one's regulated state available for others.
10. **Vocal Prosody** – Uses tone and rhythm to create calm and trust.
11. **Verbal Empathy** – Articulating the observable conditions of others.

In today's unpredictable, high-stakes environments, leaders cannot rely solely on strategy or expertise. Their ability to regulate group safety—both structurally and in the moment—determines whether their teams remain engaged, adaptive, and resilient under pressure. Those who master these skills build teams that thrive in complexity rather than succumb to it.

Toolbox Summary

After-Action Review (AAR)

Purpose: To reframe failure as a learning opportunity and foster a culture of continuous improvement.

Steps:

1. What really happened?

   - Build a shared understanding of events by integrating diverse perspectives.

2. What insights did we gain?

   - Reflect on what worked, what didn't, and why, without assigning blame.

3. How can we improve next time?

   - Turn insights into actionable strategies for future improvement.

Training Summary:

Leaders should model vulnerability by sharing their own failures and lessons learned. Conduct AARs after key projects or milestones, ensuring the focus remains on learning rather than blame. Use the three core questions to guide structured yet flexible discussions.

Crumple & Toss[6]

Purpose: To create a safe, anonymous space for team members to share concerns and ideas.

Steps:

1. **Preparation**:

   - Distribute half-sheets of paper and ask participants to write responses to:
     - "What concerns or issues are preventing progress?"
     - "What needs to happen for the group to move forward?"

2. **Crumple & Toss**:

   - Participants crumple their papers and toss them into a central area or bucket.

3. **Reading Aloud**:

   - Each participant picks a random paper and reads it aloud without commenting.

4. **Pattern Recognition**:

   - Identify recurring themes or patterns in the responses.

5. **Solution-Focused Discussion**:

   - Collaborate on actionable solutions to address the surfaced concerns.

PACE Strengths

Purpose: To build trust and engagement by focusing on team strengths rather than weaknesses.

Steps:

- **Safety Pre-frame & Ensure Commitment**:
  - Set a positive tone by checking in with participants and ensuring they feel comfortable sharing.

- **Lead with Strengths, Pre-frame Weaknesses**:
  - Highlight team strengths and frame past challenges as learning experiences.

- **Let Them Tell Their Story**:
  - Encourage free-flowing storytelling about team journeys, successes, and turning points.

- **Learning & Understanding**:
  - Reflect on insights and identify opportunities for systemic improvement.

Training Summary:

Use this approach to boost morale and cohesion. Focus on what's working well, and frame weaknesses as opportunities for growth. Ensure the conversation feels natural and energising[7].

PACE Surfacing

Purpose: To uncover hidden team intelligence and cultural dynamics through storytelling.

Steps:

1. **Grounding & Framing Contributions**:
   - Create a safe space for storytelling by using humour and non-verbal cues to signal trust.

2. **Removing Barriers to Authenticity**:
   - Normalise subjectivity and ensure participants feel free to share without fear of judgment.

3. **Letting Stories Emerge Naturally**:
   - Allow conversations to meander, focusing on resonance rather than consensus.

4. **Turning Patterns into Insights**:
   - Identify recurring themes and use them to inform actionable strategies.

Training Summary:

Use this technique to uncover tacit knowledge and cultural insights. Avoid forcing conclusions; instead, let stories reveal weak signals and hidden patterns[8].

Gold Seam Mining

Purpose: To systematically uncover, refine, and institutionalise team strengths.

Steps:

1. **Prospecting**:
    - Identify team strengths by asking questions like:
        - "What do we consistently do well, even under pressure?"
        - "What strengths give us a competitive edge?"

2. **Excavation**:
    - Analyse why these strengths exist and how they function.
    - Encourage storytelling to uncover patterns and formulas for success.

3. **Refining**:
    - Codify strengths into principles and embed them into daily practices.
    - Shift the culture to view mistakes as stepping stones to mastery.

4. **Distribution**:
    - Spread strengths across the organisation through mentorship, cross-functional sharing, and training programs.

Training Summary:

Use this structured approach to transform local successes into scalable, repeatable practices. Focus on amplifying strengths rather than fixing deficits.

Observation Skills

Breathing Patterns – Observing breath patterns to gauge emotional states and using deep breathing exercises to regulate team energy.

Goal: To regulate emotional states by observing and adjusting breathing patterns.

1. **Observe** – Watch for shallow, high-chest breathing (stress) vs. deep, abdominal breathing (relaxation).
2. **Calibrate** – Identify baseline breathing patterns for each team member.
3. **Adjust Your Own Breathing** – Before key interactions, take slow, deep breaths into your abdomen.
4. **Model & Mirror** – Consciously slow your own breath to encourage the team to unconsciously match your rhythm.
5. **Co-Regulation** – Using one's emotional stability to influence and regulate the collective emotional state of the team.

Group Dynamics – Reading team rapport and cohesion through reactions to light-hearted interactions or challenging topics[9].

Goal: To use tone and rhythm to create a psychologically safe atmosphere.

1. **Check Your Voice** – Record yourself speaking under stress vs. relaxed; listen to your natural rhythm.
2. **Slow Down Your Speech** – Avoid rushed delivery; take pauses between key points.
3. **Lower Your Pitch Slightly** – A lower, steady tone signals authority and reassurance.
4. **Soften Your Cadence** – Use a rhythmic, melodic flow rather than a flat, monotone delivery.

Conversational Skills

Vocal Prosody – Using modulation in pitch, tone, and rhythm to create a calming and reassuring environment[10].

Goal: To use tone and rhythm to create a psychologically safe atmosphere.

1. **Slow Down Your Speech** – Avoid rushed delivery; take pauses between key points.
2. **Lower Your Pitch Slightly** – A lower, steady tone signals authority and reassurance.
3. **Soften Your Cadence** – Use a rhythmic, melodic flow rather than a flat, monotone delivery.
4. **Charismatic Pattern** – A blend of up-and-down tones within the command-tone-down patterns
5. **Verbal Empathy** – Matching the intensity of team members' emotions in language to deepen engagement and create psychological safety.

Goal: To reflect emotions back accurately and make people feel understood[11].

1. **Listen Closely** – Pay attention to **exact words** and **emotional intensity**.
2. **Identify Their Emotional Language** – Are they using strong metaphors? ("I feel like I'm drowning" vs. "I'm struggling").
3. **Match Their Wording** – Echo their metaphor back ("Drowning... just trying to keep your head above water?").
4. **Watch for Recognition** – If they nod or relax, you've signalled true understanding.
5. **Move to Problem-Solving** – Once rapport is built, guide them toward constructive next steps.

PART TWO
MICRO-SKILLS FOR LEADERS

INTRODUCTION

*The strength of the pack is the wolf,
and the strength of the wolf is the pack*
Rudyard Kipling

Leadership is often considered as the art of persuasion—a well-timed speech, a clever argument, a compelling narrative. Yet beneath the surface of eloquent words and polished rhetoric lies a more potent force: the unspoken. Non-verbal communication—gestures, posture, facial expressions, and tone—shapes how we are perceived long before we speak[1]. It is the elusive language that either reinforces or undermines every word we utter.

Picture a leader walking into a room. Shoulders squared, gaze steady, movements deliberate. Without saying a word, they command attention and set the tone for what follows. Now think of that same leader entering with slouched shoulders, eyes darting anxiously, and a restless shuffle. The room senses it instantly: uncertainty. Doubt spreads before any words are spoken. This is the quiet truth of leadership—our bodies speak louder and faster than our voices ever can.

This instinctive response to non-verbal cues is not a recent phenomenon. It is ancient, embedded deep in our evolutionary wiring[2]. Long before language shaped human societies, survival depended on reading physical signals—tense muscles, a sharp glance, a subtle shift in posture. These cues conveyed threat or safety, dominance or submission. Our ancestors survived by swiftly interpreting these signs and reacting accordingly. Today, those same instincts remain, guiding how we perceive authority, trustworthiness, and confidence. In a boardroom or a meeting hall, when a leader falters in their voice or avoids eye contact, it stirs the same unease that once warned of hidden predators. The threats have changed, but the instincts have not.

At the core of non-verbal leadership is *congruence*—the alignment of what we say and how we say it. When a leader speaks of certainty but their posture sags or their voice wavers, the disconnect is palpable. People trust what they feel more than the words they hear. In contrast, congruence—where voice, posture, and expression reinforce the message—amplifies authority. A leader presenting a bold vision with steady breath, deliberate gestures, and calm confidence silently says:

"I believe this, and so should you"

Yet non-verbal communication is a double-edged sword. It is our most powerful tool and our greatest vulnerability. Words can be rehearsed, but the body reveals the truth. A clenched jaw betrays frustration. A fleeting glance exposes doubt. Mastering leadership, therefore, begins with mastering the self[3]. Before we can influence others, we must first become aware of what we unconsciously project[4].

This part explores that journey—from understanding the foundations of non-verbal influence to refining and mastering its subtle techniques. Chapter Four, *The Elusive Obvious*, uncovers the hidden power of non-verbal cues in leadership. Chapter Five, *Non-Verbal Acuity*, offers practical strategies to sharpen these signals and align them with intent. Chapter Six, *The Subtle Skillset*, delves deeper into advanced techniques—how to harness pauses, synchronise breath with speech, and manage presence under pressure. Together, these chapters offer an enlightening guide to the wordless art of leadership.

In a world awash with words, it is easy to overlook what is left unsaid. But true leadership is not about abandoning speech—it is about enriching it. The leader who masters non-verbal communication gains more than a skill; they gain presence. They move beyond words into the deeper realm of human connection. They become a leader not only heard but felt.

Much of what follows in this section stands on the shoulders of a quiet master. Michael Grinder's work on non-verbal influence was the first to show me that leadership isn't performed through words alone—it's shaped in the pauses, the posture, the moment a group inhales together. His approach made the elusive obvious. The subtle signal work you'll find in these pages is my attempt to translate his clarity into today's language of trust and team coherence.

We shall now step beyond language and into the primal power that shapes influence, builds trust and defines leadership.

FOUR
THE ELUSIVE OBVIOUS

Eyes are vocal, and they do speak
Anna Katharine Green

HOW MUCH IS SAID without uttering a word? A firm handshake, a subtle nod, the way someone enters a room—these silent actions reverberate far more than we often realise. Indeed, the words we speak are merely the tip of the iceberg. Beneath the surface, there is a far richer communication channel at play: the world of *non-verbal communication*. This elusive reality is what often determines the success or failure of our leadership interactions, as much as the words we say.

This is not to suggest that words lack importance, but rather to highlight that much of our instinctual reaction to leaders comes not from what they say, but from the myriad of signals they give off unconsciously. As leaders, we need to understand the power of the unspoken and harness it deliberately to lead effectively.

· · ·

EVOLUTIONARY ROOTS

Why do we react so powerfully to non-verbal cues? The answer lies deep in our evolutionary past. Long before the invention of language, our ancestors relied on body language and facial expressions to navigate social dynamics, signal intent, and detect threats.

As an example, 'bid' is a small snippet of behaviour designed to reaffirm connection and, by extension, safety. Picture a quick glance by someone with which you instantly react with a smile or a nod. Mammals give one another bids because it is a part of our social engagement apparatus. Reptiles do not do bids.

Picture early humans gathering around a fire, wary of predators lurking in the shadows. A raised eyebrow, a tense posture—these were often the first clues to approaching danger or the intent of a rival. The ability to quickly interpret these signals was essential for survival.

Fast forward to the modern office or boardroom, and those ancient instincts remain. Think of someone more powerful than you, or someone you regard as an ally. You're on the other side of a busy room from them. You make casual eye contact and nod—but you don't receive a reciprocal gesture. Your gut reacts as though something is wrong.

Mammals evolved with a safety sense that required sufficient cues of safety to be triggered: an apparent absence of danger was not enough. After all, there were an assortment of apex predators and poisonous creepy-crawlies, not to mention other humans, hiding waiting to strike. *Nothingness is somethingness* to our neuroception's threat detection.

OK, the threats are no longer sabertoothed tigers but the social risks—losing trust, missing opportunities, appearing weak—are still very real. Our brains are hardwired to read non-verbal cues faster than words. Non-reciprocation is a non-verbal cue as much as how confidently a person carry themselves.

To be a leader who commands respect and trust, we must acknowledge these instinctual mechanisms and learn to control the non-verbal messages we send. *It's not just what you say that matters—it's what you do and don't do.*

Case Story: Instinctual Leadership

Consider the case of Bruce, a logistics operations lead, as he enters a critical meeting with his team. The stakes are high; the project is behind schedule, and Bruce needs to regain control. As he steps into the room, before he has the chance to speak, a wealth of non-verbal communication is already occurring.

Bruce's confident stride, the square set of his shoulders, and his open, relaxed posture send immediate signals of authority. His instinctual leadership begins the moment he steps through the door. Without saying a word, he projects competence and control. His team, sensing this, subconsciously adjusts their own posture, mirroring his energy and preparing for a productive discussion.

THAT's what *actually* happened but consider the counterfactual: Bruce enters the room with slouched shoulders, his gaze darting nervously around the table. He fidgets with his notes and avoids eye contact. The message is clear, even if it is unintended: Bruce is uncertain. And his team, picking up on these non-verbal cues, starts to feel uneasy. Trust in his leadership begins to erode, and before the meeting even begins, the dynamics are set against him.

The contrast in these two scenarios highlights how much leadership is conveyed non-verbally.

> *It's not what you say, it's how you say it—and more importantly, how you carry yourself when you say it.*

Projecting Non-Verbal Cues

The significance of non-verbal communication in leadership cannot be overstated. Our brains are tuned to pick up on subtle cues—facial expressions, posture, gestures—that influence how we perceive others. In fact, research consistently shows that up to *93% of the communication of emotions and attitudes are non-verbal*. If this statistic sounds staggering, it is because we tend to underestimate how much of our day-to-day interactions are driven by signals, we barely notice.

Let's break down some of the key components of non-verbal communication:

- *Body Language*: A leader's posture, gestures, and movement can signal confidence, openness, or defensiveness. Standing tall with open gestures conveys confidence and approachability, whereas crossed arms or slouched posture signals uncertainty or closed-off attitudes.
- *Facial Expressions*: The human face is capable of over 10,000 expressions, and even subtle changes can drastically alter how someone is perceived. A smile can disarm tension, while a furrowed brow can create discomfort. In shutdown and freeze states, the human face becomes flat and impassive, which might elude all but the most observant. As a leader, controlling your facial expressions is crucial in managing how others experience your presence.

- *Eye Contact*: Direct eye contact is one of the most powerful tools in a leader's arsenal. It signals attentiveness, trust and connection. Avoiding eye contact can convey disinterest or insecurity, which can undermine authority and rapport.
- *Tone of Voice*: The way something is said often matters more than the content. A calm, measured tone instils confidence, while a shaky or high-pitched voice can convey anxiety, even if the words being spoken are logical.

These cues are processed in an instant by those around us. And unlike spoken words, non-verbal cues are often unconscious and difficult to fake. Therefore, as a leader, controlling these signals—making them congruent with your words—is essential for effective communication.

Tips for Leaders

Now that we understand the critical role of non-verbal congruence, the next question is how can leaders improve their non-verbal skills? Here are some practical tips:

- *Awareness:* Start by becoming more aware of your non-verbal cues. Consider recording yourself in meetings or presentations and then review the footage to see how you come across. Are your gestures open? Is your posture confident? Awareness is the first step to improvement.
- *Posture:* Focus on standing tall with your shoulders back and chest open. Good posture signals confidence and authority. Avoid slumping or crossing your arms, as these can be interpreted as defensive or unsure.
- *Eye Contact:* Make a conscious effort to maintain eye contact, especially when delivering important messages.

Direct eye contact builds trust and makes your audience feel seen and heard.
- *Tone and Volume*: Practice modulating your voice. Speak slowly and clearly, with a steady tone. Varying your volume to emphasise key points can also keep your audience engaged and convey confidence.
- *Controlled Breathing*: Your breathing pattern affects your voice and overall energy. Deep, steady breathing calms the body and mind, helping you project confidence and control.

By consciously controlling these aspects of non-verbal communication, you can greatly enhance your effectiveness as a leader. Remember:

People may forget what you said, but they will remember how you made them feel.

And much of that feeling comes from your non-verbal communication.

THE ELUSIVE REALITY of non-verbal communication plays a pivotal role in how you are perceived and, ultimately, how successful you are. It is not enough to speak well; you must also present yourself in a way that aligns with your words. By mastering the art of non-verbal communication, you can project confidence, build trust, and lead with greater authority. In the next chapter, we will explore how to refine and perfect these skills through specific techniques, allowing you to master the subtle but powerful world of non-verbal leadership.

FIVE
NON-VERBAL ACUITY

A gesture cannot be regarded as the expression of a sentiment, which is meant to remain internal; it must be understood as a kind of declaration which tries to express itself publicly
Marcel Mauss

NON-VERBAL COMMUNICATION? As we explored in the previous chapter, it plays both a central and critical role in leadership. Now, it's time to move from theory into practice. Developing of non-verbal skills requires not only awareness but also the deliberate and thoughtful application of these tools in real-world situations. Just as a conductor wields subtle gestures to evoke harmony from an orchestra, a leader must use their body, voice, and presence to orchestrate an environment of trust, authority, and collaboration.

CASE STORY: Non-Verbal Fumble

Let's examine two scenes that illustrate the power of a leader's body language. Picture Angus, the Managing Director of a supply chain business, announcing a major company culture change initiatives to one of his large distribution team called, *'Values & Behaviours'*.

The shop floor workforce is known for their irreverence to authority, which is one of the reasons for the new policy to begin with. Angus has prepared a detailed presentation, explaining the rationale and benefits of the change, a summary copy of which is placed on each chair prior to the meeting.

As he begins to speak, his non-verbal cues were telling:

- His shoulders are slightly hunched, suggesting tension or uncertainty.
- His gripping the podium tightly, his knuckles white with strain.
- His eyes dart around the room rather than making steady eye contact.
- His voice, though he is trying to sound confident, has a slight quaver.

Despite the carefully crafted words of his presentation, Angus's non-verbal cues are broadcasting uncertainty and anxiety. The workforce, picking up on these unconscious signals, begin to grumble and gesticulate about the proposed changes. They realise that they are about to have their wings clipped. As Angus continued to speak, the workforce started to point to their handouts and discuss things amongst themselves.

This makes Angus feel disrespected and embarrassed. Once he begins to blush, he stops talking and glares at the workforce. In shrill high-pitched voice, Angus demands respectful silence whilst he is speaking. Of course, this makes him appear flaky and, true to reputation, the audience is watching the spectacle in quiet grinning satisfaction.

Angus picks up the pace and, with the armpits of his blue business shirt wet with sweat, he gets through to the end of the presentation. When asked if there were any question, there were none. He thanks them for their time and permits them to return to work. Once the room emptied, only a few summaries were left behind—some on the chairs, others flopped onto the floor.

So, that is what *actually* happened. However, consider an alternative reality, where Angus walks in with an upright, relaxed posture. He makes warm eye contact with team members as he welcomes everyone. He walks around shaking hands with people and acknowledging people he knows. His gestures are open and inclusive. His voice is steady, rich and resonant. He makes a few humorous remarks at his own expense that has everyone laughing together. Even before he delves into the details of the presentation, Angus's non-verbal communication has already sent a powerful message of confidence and reassurance.

In both versions, the content of Angus message is identical. But the non-verbal packaging dramatically alters how his words are received and interpreted by his team's instinctual brains. So, let's start to break down the elements of non-verbal cues and communication.

Points of Focus *in Communication*

Much like how sailors use the terms "port" and "starboard" to orient themselves in any direction, leaders can use distinct *points of focus* in communication to direct attention with precision. Understanding where to direct your focus—and that of your audience—can make or break the outcome of an interaction.

Here are four key points of focus that every leader should understand:

- **One-point**: This is when the leader focuses inward, looking down at themselves or their internal experience. Think of it as the introspective mode, where you are reflecting or gathering your thoughts. Leaders often use this when they pause to consider their next words carefully.
- **Two-point**: The leader makes *direct eye contact* with the person they're addressing. This is where rapport is built, where trust is established. Two-point focus is especially effective in one-on-one conversations or small meetings where personal connection is essential.
- **Three-point**: Both the leader and the listener direct their attention to an external *third point*, such as a document or a shared visual aid. This is particularly useful for discussing complex or sensitive topics, as it allows for a collaborative, less confrontational approach. It shifts the focus from being personal to being task oriented.
- **Four-point**: This is when the leader directs their focus to something outside the immediate conversation—perhaps *into the distance* or at an abstract point beyond the present moment. It's often used when discussing larger ideas, the future, or something conceptual. Leaders use four-point focus when they want to take the audience beyond the immediate and make them consider broader possibilities.

Example in Action:

Bruce is leading a discussion on a new project, *'Balancing Outbound Volumes'*, which is aimed at equalising the outbound volumes over several distribution centres. During the discussion, Bruce focuses on a three-point—a PowerPoint presentation to which he is gesturing to clarify the logistics.

But when the conversation shifts to the project's broader impact on the company's future, he adopts a four-point focus, gesturing outward as if to encompass larger ideas, pulling the team into a vision of what the future could hold. This shift subtly signals to the audience that they are moving from detail-oriented work to visionary thinking.

Peripheral Awareness

Peripheral awareness is another critical skill. Leaders must gauge their audience's reactions, even when not making direct eye contact. Sometimes cultural norms or specific situations discourage direct eye contact, but a leader can still be attuned to the room using peripheral vision. *Peripheral awareness* allows you to sense the energy, mood, and reactions of others without staring directly at them, which can be useful in tense negotiations or when speaking to a larger crowd.

Non-Verbal Behavioural Clusters

On a spectrum of non-verbal behavioural clusters, at one end there are *approachable* clusters of behaviour and, on the other, there are *credible* clusters of behaviour . The approachable cluster is typified with a movement, such as a bobbing head, swaying body, an angled posture and gesticulation; facial expressions, such as smiling and raised eyebrows; and a modulating voice pattern and upward inflexions. These behaviours signal safety and send an autonomic invitation to connect. A friendly flight attendant is the poster child for this cluster.

The credible cluster is typified with stillness, minimal facial expression, zero gesticulation, an upright posture, with a flat voice tone that turns down at the end of sentences. A great example of this would be an airline pilot, the poster child of which is Captain Sullenberger, who was played by Tom Hanks in the movie 'Sully'. His emotionless narrative as he pilots a plane full of passengers into the Hudson River is remarkable. It connotes safety due to perceived intelligence and competence.

As a thought experiment, imagine the flight attendant with the credible cluster, with complete stillness, zero facial expression and flat voice welcoming you aboard. Or a highly energised up-and-downy voice coming over the 'tannoy' excitingly telling you about the potential for bad weather and turbulence. I'm sure that you will find them comically incongruent with their new situations.

Whilst these clusters are polar categories, they do give us clues on how we can modify our own non-verbals to be congruent for our teams given the different circumstances in which we find ourselves. In circumstances that benefit from a more cool, cognitive or sober approach, dialling up our inner 'Sully' would be highly advantageous. Reviewing and evaluating an important proposition, talking to the facts of an investigation or addressing people during an emergency are all times where we benefit the listener with increased credibility.

At the same time, in circumstances where a higher degree of energy, enthusiasm, empathy or human connection, dialling up our friendly flight attendant would better suit the moment. Meeting someone at a networking event, lightening the start of an interview or ending a meeting on an upbeat note are all example of where we benefit the listeners with increased approachability.

Eye-Hand Coordination

Effective leaders not only direct focus with their eyes but also with their hands. *Eye-hand coordination* helps guide the audience's attention to where the leader wants it to go. For example, if a leader gestures towards a specific point, synchronising their gaze with the movement of their hand, it creates a more powerful and cohesive message.

But there's a subtle art to this. There are two primary methods of gesturing that can shape how a leader is perceived:

1. *Bouncing the hand towards a point*: the movement makes the leader seem more approachable, encouraging a sense of openness.
2. *Holding the hand steady and vertical*: This communicates authority, signalling that the leader's message is serious and definitive.

The difference between these two gestures can change the atmosphere in a room. A bouncing hand invites dialogue; a steady hand commands attention.

Breath & Perception

The voice is an instrument, and breath is the bow that brushes over the vocal folds. Together, they shape how your message is perceived. A voice that is steady and aligned with controlled breathing carries authority; a voice paired with shallow, erratic breathing often projects insecurity or stress.

Breathing patterns directly influence vocal tone. When you breathe deeply, your voice resonates with warmth and steadiness. Shallow breathing, by contrast, produces a higher, more strained pitch, which can inadvertently signal nervousness or irritation.

Non-verbally, each pairing of tone and breathing creates a different perception to the observer:

- *Low Breathing + Approachable*: Signals warmth and reliability.
- *Low Breathing + Credible*: Conveys intelligence, authority, and composure.
- *High Breathing + Approachable*: Comes across as flaky or insincere.
- *High Breathing + Credible*: Risks being interpreted as hostile or impatient.

In the unlikely event that you want to be perceived as hostile, impatient, insincere or flaky, before addressing your team, take a moment to autoregulate yourself. Once you are breathing low, you are in the right state to project a positive emotional echo. If you aim to inspire trust, combine low, steady breathing with a measured, approachable undulations, throwing in a smile and flowy gestures. If you need to project clear authority, use the same low breathing, show less facial expression, be more still, and have flatter undulations with command-down intonation.

Your non-verbals are a vehicle for your message, but your breath pattern can support or undermine your communication. By practicing the interplay of these elements, you can align your intent with your impact, ensuring your communication resonates deeply with your audience.

Non-verbal skills require practice and awareness. Leaders who understand how to direct focus, modulate their voice, and engage with the room through subtle cues become far more effective in inspiring trust and authority. As with any skill, the more you practice, the more natural it becomes, allowing you to communicate effortlessly without needing to overthink the mechanics. In the next chapter, we will explore how to harness the power of the pause and breathing techniques to deepen your non-verbal influence.

SIX
THE SUBTLE SKILLSET

Art is the imposing of a pattern on experience,
and our aesthetic enjoyment is recognition of the pattern
Alfred North Whitehead

LEADERSHIP GOES BEYOND WORDS. It is created from gestures, silences, and the breath between sentences. See a leader entering a room where tension hangs like a storm cloud. Without raising their voice or uttering more than a word, they exude calm authority. Their movements are deliberate, their pauses resonate with meaning, and their breath—steady and measured—sets the rhythm of engagement.

Non-verbal communication is the silent language of influence. It wields more power than is often credited. From the depth of our breathing to the spaces between our words, non-verbal cues shape how others perceive us. These subtle signals determine whether we are trusted, respected, or dismissed.

In this chapter, we explore how to master the unspoken elements of communication. You'll learn to control the emotional atmosphere through breathing, punctuate your words with purposeful pauses, and align your voice with your intent. These are not mere techniques; they are tools to craft a leadership presence that inspires trust, amplifies authority, and fosters genuine connection.

By the end, you will see how silence, breath, and voice are not empty spaces or fleeting sounds—they are the scaffolding upon which skilled leaders build their influence.

CASE STORY: **Negotiation Success**

Let's take a closer look at Karen, a senior executive entrusted with negotiating a major contract for her firm. The stakes are high, and her counterpart—a seasoned negotiator—is known for dominating discussions with fast-paced, assertive speech. Karen feels the pressure mounting but recalls her preparation: she knows that controlling the flow of conversation without appearing confrontational will be key.

As the negotiation begins, Karen feels her pulse quicken. She instinctively wants to respond immediately to counter her opponent's aggressive tone. Instead, she pauses. She takes a slow, deliberate breath, grounding herself. The silence stretches, compelling her counterpart to lean back slightly, caught off guard by the unexpected stillness. Karen uses this pause to process the argument presented and carefully shape her response.

Karen takes a rapid *Dual-Mind Reflection** and, using her internal dialogue, says:

"*Stay composed. Own this silence. Let them fill it*".

She consciously relaxes her shoulders, steadying her breath. The

---

* Dual-Mind Reflection is the process of calming the body and assess a decision rationally—review facts, evidence, and pros and cons. Then, tune into gut feelings and physical sensations, as these can reveal deeper, non-verbal cues. Balance logic and instinct: if they align, proceed. See':

O'Neill, P. '*The Inner Game of Leadership*', Lantern & Light Press, 2025.

negotiation is no longer a verbal tug-of-war but a dance of controlled energy. Her deep, measured breathing sends subtle signals of confidence and control. She notices her counterpart beginning to slow down, mirroring her calm pace.

As the discussion intensifies, Karen's internal dialogue keeps her balanced:

"Breathe. Listen. Respond with clarity".

She poses thoughtful, open-ended questions and waits patiently for answers. The once dominant negotiator grows more reflective, unsettled by Karen's composure. The tension in the room slowly dissolves, replaced by a steady rhythm of dialogue.

By the meeting's end, Karen has secured favourable terms for her firm. Her success wasn't rooted in aggressive tactics but in the quiet strength of deliberate pauses and controlled breathing. Her poised presence turned a potentially combative negotiation into a collaborative exchange. Karen left the room not only with a signed contract but with her reputation solidified as a negotiator who commands respect without raising her voice.

Leadership Breathing

Just as pauses can control the tempo of a conversation, breathing can control the emotional energy in the room. Deep, steady breathing helps leaders manage their own stress, while simultaneously influencing the emotional state of those around them.

When *probing for permission*, one very effective visual cue is 'BLIP' (Breathing Low Indicates Permission). We can use this insight to infer whether someone has given us permission. At the same time, when a leader breathes deeply, it sends an autonomic invitation to 'approach and connect'. It's the 'welcome' mat on your front step. Conversely, shallow, high breathing signals an autonomic warning 'I am danger. Stay away'. It's the 'beware of the dog' sign on your fence. Others can pick up on, often unconsciously, and will connect or disconnect, accordingly.

Let's explore two ways leaders can use breathing to their advantage:

1. *Managing Personal Stress*: When under pressure, the instinct is often to breathe rapidly and shallowly, which can increase stress. By consciously breathing deeply and slowly, leaders can activate the body's parasympathetic nervous system, which promotes relaxation and reduces the effects of stress hormones like cortisol.
2. *Influencing Others*: People tend to mirror the body language and breathing patterns of those around them. When a leader breathes calmly and deeply, their mirror neurons induces others to do the same. This can be particularly useful in tense meetings or during difficult conversations. If the leader remains calm, it helps create a more relaxed atmosphere for everyone involved.

Example: Think of a leader entering a tense meeting where emotions are running high. By focusing on their breathing—taking slow, deep breaths—they not only keep their own nerves in check but also influence the breathing patterns of their team. As the leader speaks, the team members, noticing the calm, begin to mirror this slower, more relaxed pace. The atmosphere shifts from one of tension to one of constructive dialogue.

SILENCE PROJECTS INTELLIGENCE

Pausing during speech isn't just about giving yourself time to think—it also enhances how others perceive your intelligence. In Western cultures, pauses are often interpreted as a sign of thoughtfulness and depth. When you pause, it signals to your audience that you are considering your words carefully, which in turn makes your speech feel more deliberate and meaningful.

In fact, studies have shown that people who pause before responding are often rated as more intelligent, trustworthy and composed. This is because a pause conveys confidence—you're not rushing to fill the silence with unnecessary words. Instead, you're allowing yourself space to breathe, reflect, and respond with clarity.

But what exactly makes a pause so powerful? It comes down to a few key elements:

1. *Visual*: During a pause, remain still with your mouth closed. Movement during a pause can signal nervousness or uncertainty. Breathing through your mouth reduces your *perceived intelligence*. So, hold your posture confidently, breathe through your nose and make direct eye contact.
2. *Auditory*: Silence is golden during a pause. Don't rush to fill the space with filler words like "um" or "ah." Let the silence speak for itself.
3. *Kinaesthetic*: Stay grounded. Keep your weight evenly balanced on both feet and avoid shifting or fidgeting. Your body language should reflect that you are in control of the moment.

When done effectively, a pause can raise your perceived intelligence quotient and reinforce your authority. It gives the impression that every word you utter has been carefully considered, which in turn elevates the impact of your message.

Getting Attention Professionally

See yourself walking into a crowded room, the air buzzing with conversation. Laughter ripples through pockets of chatter, and the hum of voices fills every corner. It's time for you to give a speech, a briefing or make an announcement. As a leader, you must first earn the attention of the group before guiding them anywhere. And this begins with how you address them.

Your opening sets the tone, letting everyone know you have something important to share. So, start strong - with pulse of volume that is sufficient to punch through the loud rumbling hum of conversation and noise.

The bigger group or the louder the noise, the louder the vocal pulse of volume required. The smaller the group, the quieter the noise, the softer the pulse of volume needed. In either case, you're aiming for brevity, clarity and authority; because the important thing is not what you say but the way that you say it. Indeed, it could be as simple as, "Good morning!"

Once you have their attention, stop. Let the silence linger for two or three beats. This isn't hesitation—it's strategy. A deliberate *pause* is like the steady draw of breath before a leap, charged with energy and anticipation. While you pause, scan the room. Look at your audience calmly and purposefully. This moment of quiet creates intrigue and signals that what comes next is worth hearing. You've caught their full attention, now allow them to approach and connect with you.

When you begin to speak, *lower your voice*, as though you're sharing a secret that everyone in the room needs to hear. In smaller spaces, speak just below a conversational volume; in larger ones, ensure your voice still carries softly enough to make people lean in to listen. This shift from *strong to silence to soft* draws the audience closer with intent. It makes your message feel intimate and profound.

Competent vocal dynamics transforms the way you connect with others. A strong voice grabs attention; a pause builds anticipation; and a whisper draws people closer, creating a powerful rhythm that prevents monotony. This is Michael Grinder's *"ABOVE (Pause) Whisper"* technique. It is a beautifully crafted sequence by a master influencer. It taps into human instinct, where changes in tone signal importance and evoke emotion.

Tense Conversations

In 2006, I stood before seven hundred and fifty employees to deliver the words they feared most: they were being made redundant. Rumours had rippled through the workforce for weeks, softening the blow only in theory. Yet, when spoken aloud, the confirmation struck hard. To my left, a large screen displayed a summary of the plan. Blue background, deep yellow lettering—an intentional choice for clarity in the mottled light of the hall. Every phrase I spoke had been crafted with care, every pause deliberately placed to give the weight of the words room to settle.

I told them the site would close after a five-week inventory rundown. I explained that the decision was final, irreversible. For most, that very day would be their last. The remaining few would stay to wind things down. My voice was slow, measured. I spoke with a prosodic calm designed not to soothe in a patronising way, but to give them space to think, to breathe, to understand.

As I spoke, I watched it happen—that quiet moment when comprehension turns cold and heavy. Bodies stilled. Faces slackened. Eyes fixed not on me but on the slides behind me, as though hoping the text might contradict what their ears had heard. It was easy, almost painfully so, to think of the mental arithmetic each person was performing. Mortgage payments. School fees. Pensions. Futures rearranged in an instant.

This was no gentle crowd. The workforce had a history of industrial action, and violence wasn't beyond possibility. We had security in place, discreet but ready. Yet, not once was it needed. No shouts, no threats. Only silence. A few low murmurs after I finished, the sound of people cautiously stepping back into a world that had just changed. Within twenty minutes, each person had their letter, detailing entitlements and final payments. One by one, they left. Quietly. Thoughtfully.

Outside, two news vans idled, cameras poised to catch whatever anger or despair might spill out onto the pavement. Later that night, I watched the broadcast, the reporter calling it 'sickening'. Perhaps it was, though not for the reasons they intended.

That day, I learned something critical about leadership under pressure. In volatile moments, a leader's presence can either steady the ground beneath people's feet or shake it loose entirely. We knew the psychological responses we might provoke—anger, fear, paralysis—and we planned meticulously to guide people through it. This wasn't about manipulation but about responsibility. It was our duty to carry them through that moment with dignity.

PACE Yourself...

Leadership is not just about the words we choose but how we carry ourselves when delivering them. Preparing oneself before facing a group—especially when delivering difficult news—is a profound act of respect and courtesy to those we lead. Through thorough autoregulation, we stabilise our internal state. In doing so, we honour the emotional weight our audience must bear, ensuring that our own unregulated emotions do not spill over and burden them further. This is where the PACE Protocol supports not just our resilience but our ethical leadership.

To stand before a group and guide them through challenging news requires more than information—it requires presence, steadiness, and empathy. Leaders must first extend the principles of the PACE Protocol inward, grounding themselves so they can responsibly guide others through moments of volatility.

... to Lead

Too often, leaders rush into difficult situations half-prepared, weighed down by doubt or distraction. This unfocused, scattered mental state is unacceptable. Instead, a deliberate internal check-in reframes the moment:

> *"Have I given myself full permission to speak with compassion, precision and credibility?"*

This self-questioning is not indulgence—it is responsibility. If you cannot answer in the affirmative, you need to do the 'Inner Game' work. At the point of delivery is no place for the 'impostor syndrome' or public speaking anxieties. Your duty is to be autonomically regulated to be able to step fully into the role of *guide*, ready to carry both the message and its emotional consequences. If you are struggling to get there by yourself, accept it and seek coaching and support.

This is important because, in moments of high stress, our instinct is to fight, flight or freeze. Yet leadership demands grounded, credible and effective responses. Before and during the engagement, ask yourself:

> *"Is my next action driven by instinct, intuition or thoughtful choice?"*

This simple question interrupts the automatic patterns that can derail effective communication. This pause is not hesitation, nor will it be perceived as such. It is an invitation to a Dual-Mind Reflection and it will be perceived as self-control. It is the conscious decision to respond with Primate purpose rather than Reptile reflex.

And, whilst leaders must learn to control themselves, leadership is not about control. It is about connection. However, stress severs connection and locks us in survival mode. As people mirror their leaders, we must ensure our bodies are transmitting *autonomic invitations* to 'approach and connect'. Ask:

> *"Am I feeling good with full access my social engagement behaviours?"*

This ensures that the leader has primed their own safety. By doing so, they are emotionally available to the group, capable of meeting them where they are and leading them forward.

Neuro-resilience is not an improvised accident. Rather, it is prepared for through practice and contemplating future with a problem-solver's mindset.

> *"What scenarios can I mentally prepare for to stay composed and present?"*

This question needs to be answered thoroughly. However, most leaders and influencers fail to give it its due diligence. They believe that, once they've written their speech or presentation, or pulled together their support material for their difficult discussion, that they're done. They are not. Mentally rehearsing successful outcomes means integrating new learnings and understandings in a useful way.

In the PACE Protocol, we refer to this as *embedding* new insights and strategies. These strategies can be new inner game patterns of thinking and feeling. They can be *outer game* observational, conversational and behavioural patterns. They can be verbal and non-verbal patterns. Its purpose is to get the speaker's particular brain and body ready to deliver a particular message to a particular group, in a way that best maintains the accuracy of the information and the safety of all parties. This is so important that I shall reprise 'Preparing to Win' at the end of the chapter

... for Bad News

So, before engaging in a challenging conversation, it's essential to centre oneself within the framework of the *PACE Protocol*. After ensuring that you have given yourself full permission to have a successful (if challenging) encounter, check in with your instinct/cognition status with a *Dual-Mind Reflection*.

Instinct (Thinking Fast)	Cognition (Thinking Slow)
• Rapid pattern recognition • Driven by experience • Quick, intuitive decisions • Effective in familiar contexts • Emotionally charged reactions	• Analytical reasoning • Deliberate and logical • Time-consuming decisions • Mitigates emotional biases • Effective in novel situations

Here a quick and effective technique that Michael Grinder calls: *Break & Breathe Twice*:

- *Break*: Snap out of the negative state into which you are going. changing your physiology is a highly effective way of

doing this: shift your position by standing up, or sitting back, or look in another direction, etc.; then
- *Breathe*: Take two deep, intentional breaths. Regain your mental clarity, your cognition and inner calm.

I have found this to be a very practical technique with which to assert *agency* over instinct before, during and after difficult encounters. I like it, first, because it's simple: you're breathing anyway, so breathing a little differently on purpose is an easy way to exercise personal agency over one's instinctual *autonomic nervous system*. Second, in meetings, it is a quick, covert and low concentration technique.

Either way, the technique allows me to easily phase-transition into *connection* by applying one or more techniques from 'The Inner Game of Leadership'. For me that's 'spinning a good feeling' – calm, jovial, fascinated. Then I engage my peripheral vision, which keeps me alert to what's happening around me, regardless of on what I am focused.

That's what I do. Try it for yourself. If it doesn't work for you, ditch it. If it works OK, tweak it, so it works better. The point isn't doing my particular technique but finding your own 'go-to' autoregulation techniques. Whatever your recipe ends up being, my *state management* strategy prepares me to approach a challenging conversation clear headed and with my full social engagement functions available to me.

BASELINE CALIBRATING

As the conversation initiates, you are almost always going to begin in 'two-point' communication. As you do so, ensure you take full advantage by observing and understanding the other person's state and responses. This is done through *sensory acuity*, paying close attention to the sensory details of the other person's verbal and non-verbal cues. *Then calibrate to their state at that moment.*

If this is your first encounter, this becomes your baseline for the conversation, and you can watch for variation as the discussion progresses. This allows you to track as the other person becomes more or less socialised, mobilised or immobilised. If you already have a baseline from prior engagements, contrast (seek for differences) with how they are behaving against their baseline. Are you beginning the conversation from a point where they are more or less socialised, mobilised or immobilised than their baseline?

As always, this includes noting visual, auditory, and kinaesthetic (VAK) signals, as well as breathing patterns. By concentrating on what is genuinely happening for the other person, you remain attuned to the other's instinct–cognitive status... then comes the moment you've been (not) looking forward to... share the bad news!

How Not to Get Shot

Delivering difficult news is one of the most challenging tasks a leader faces. Missteps can erode trust, damage relationships, and escalate tension. Michael Grinder's communication technique offers a powerful solution by guiding leaders through emotionally charged conversations with greater composure and professionalism. This approach empowers both messenger and recipient, fostering understanding and collaboration even in tough moments.

Grinder's method comprises three core strategies designed to prevent defensive reactions and encourage constructive dialogue: shifting to third-person phrasing, using visual communication, and introducing a third point of focus. Together, these techniques can transform how difficult conversations unfold.

Go Third-Person: In high-stakes conversations, the words we choose can either defuse tension or intensify conflict. Using third-person phrasing, particularly through the passive voice, naturally creates a calmer, more neutral tone compared to the immediacy of first- and second-person language. This shift directs attention to the situation rather than individuals, reducing personal blame and emotional charge.

For example, saying "Respect was not maintained" focuses on the issue, whereas "I feel disrespected" or "You didn't follow the procedure" personalises the problem, often triggering defensive reactions. In tense situations, this subtle linguistic shift fosters problem-solving rather than blame.

However, leaders must balance the passive voice with active, solution-oriented statements to maintain clarity and accountability. For example, "Let's find a way to ensure procedures are followed next time" promotes collaboration without assigning blame.

Go Visual: Humans are wired to process visual information more effectively than text alone. Presenting challenging information visually—through letters, slides, or diagrams—empowers the recipient to absorb the message at their own pace. *You* control how the content is framed: plain or technical language, formal or informal tone, structured layouts, and visual aids like graphs or images.

Visual aids act as emotional anchors, engaging the analytical Primate Brain and tempering the Reptilian Brain's fight-or-flight response. In Polyvagal Theory terms, visuals support the vagal brake, sustaining social engagement behaviours. This approach promotes clarity and retention, especially for complex or emotionally sensitive information.

Consider how a financial report, presented as a clear graph rather than dense text, softens the impact of poor performance data. When recipients can revisit the information independently, they regain agency, reducing stress and emotional reactivity.

If the recipient becomes overwhelmed, cognitive function can drop by up to 35%. Allowing them to re-engage with visual material mitigates this effect, offering space for understanding and thoughtful response.

Go Three-Point: Direct eye contact during difficult conversations can intensify emotional states, whether positive or negative. Imagine two lovers sharing a gaze across candlelight, two rivals locked in a stare-down or two kids looking at one another with runaway giggles. When we lock eyes, we amplify what is between us. This is two-point communication—an intense, direct energy exchange.

Introducing a third focal point, such as a document or visual aid, diffuses this intensity. By redirecting attention to the information rather than the messenger, the emotional load is reduced. This _stabilises_ the interaction, preserving cognitive clarity and emotional balance.

Orally delivering bad news forces the recipient to depend solely on the messenger, increasing stress and reducing personal agency. Repeated clarifications can lead to the messenger becoming associated with negative emotions. Providing a shared reference point (like a handout or chart) allows both parties to engage with the content without amplifying interpersonal tension.

Ultimately, by proactively priming one's own safety first and applying Grinder's '*How Not to Get Shot*', leaders (and other messengers) remain connected, approachable and credible. In doing so, create the conditions for sound cognitive problem-solving and group collaboration, all which will lead to a more resilient future.

In turn, their team (or other recipients, like bosses, clients and peers) feel more connected, engaged and in control. Becoming competent in these strategies will not only defuse tension but also strengthen relationships and build trust. Start integrating these PACE aligned strategies into your daily practice and resilient team outcomes

... for Future Wins

Neuro-resilient rehearsal isn't about dreamy wishful thinking. It's about conditioning your mind and body to perform with clarity and confidence under pressure. By vividly pre-living a desired outcome, leaders can strengthen their emotional readiness and align their actions with their goals.

Consider how elite athletes prepare for high-stakes moments. Before ever stepping onto the field or into the ring, they have already 'lived' the victory in their minds. They visualise every detail—the sound of the crowd, the feel of the environment, the precise movements they'll execute. This mental preparation primes their nervous system and sharpens their focus, guiding their real-world actions toward that desired outcome. Champion boxer and cultural icon, Muhammed Ali, called this technique, *'Future History'*.

You can apply this same strategy to leadership. Before entering a challenging conversation or delivering difficult news, take time to mentally walk through the experience. Visualise yourself standing confidently, speaking with composure and empathy. See what you will see—the room, their faces, your slide show, your notes in your hand. Hear what you will hear—the chatter before you begin, your voice as you deliver the message, their voices asking questions and making comments. Feel what you will feel—the emotions, the sensations, your energy levels.

Then switch from two-point to four-point and witness yourself. See how you look and how you move; hear your vocal pattern, hear your words. Did you need to get their attention with an "ABOVE (pause) Whisper", was the room already deathly silent or did a cordial initial conversation morph into the main discussion?

If it is a volatile situation:

- Are you using third-party language, depersonalising your initial statements and answers to any question.
    - What questions are likely to be asked?
    - What topics must be discussed in the passive voice?
- Did you deliver the message visually?
    - Are you using handouts or individual computer devices?
    - Is there a slide show?
- Are you engaged in a three-point conversation
    - Standing in front of a group, referring to slide show off to the side?
    - Sitting at a table, at 90 degrees to the listener, using your pen to step them through the information?

This process is more than visualisation—it's strategic mental conditioning. By rehearsing success, your mind becomes attuned to recognising opportunities and responding to challenges effectively. Your actions naturally align with your preparation, making you more adaptable and resilient.

Try this practice the next time you face a difficult task:

1. *Set the Scene*: Find a quiet space and close your eyes. Imagine the setting in detail—where you'll be, who will be present, and the atmosphere in the room.
2. *Engage Your Senses*: What do you see, hear and feel in this moment? Listen to your voice calm and steady, your posture strong yet approachable.
3. *Visualise Success*: Picture yourself navigating the situation smoothly. See yourself guiding others toward the best possible outcome; hear yourself responding thoughtfully;

and feel your body moving smoothly and feel how good you feel.
4. *Anchor the Feeling*: Squeeze your thumb and index finger—because what is fired together is wired together—let your body become a resource you can draw upon.

Done well, the PACE Protocol involves very thorough *future pacing*, designed to *embed* new strategies and insight by detailed mental rehearsal, so that your desired responses flow easily and naturally in that future moment. It is another example of *agency over instinct*, as you programme yourself to feel and act differently in the future. In doing so, you are mentally preparing thoroughly to be the best version of yourself. You are not chasing perfection vainly, rather you are making sure that 'a lot of little things will be done well'.

LEADERSHIP IS OFTEN MISTAKEN for the loudest voice in the room or the sharpest command issued. Yet, as this chapter has shown, true leadership lies in mastering the subtleties—the silent pauses, the steady breath, the poised stance. These understated elements are not ancillary to leadership; they are foundational. They shape perceptions, guide emotions, and foster trust, often without a single word being spoken.

Karen's negotiation success exemplifies how a composed breath and strategic pause can shift the dynamics of power. The deliberate control of silence, the conscious modulation of voice, and the intentional use of body language are not theatrical performances but authentic expressions of authority and empathy. They are tools that signal to others:

"You are safe. We can get through this together"

In moments of high tension, it is the leader's regulated presence that can anchor a group, transforming volatility into stability. The PACE Protocol, the "Break & Breathe Twice" technique, and the strategic use of visual and third-point communication are more than techniques—they are disciplines of emotional intelligence and social mastery. They enable leaders to respond with thoughtfulness rather than react with instinct, ensuring that even the most challenging messages are delivered with dignity and clarity.

These subtle skills not only help navigate difficult situations but also elevate moments of success. They make great moments greater and bad moments better, allowing leaders to amplify celebration and soften hardship. The ability to adapt and apply these techniques across varying circumstances strengthens a leader's capacity to inspire and unify their teams.

This subtle skillset, when honed, does more than prevent miscommunication or manage conflict. It builds resilient teams, fosters emotional safety, and creates environments where people feel connected and understood. The ability to project calm, invite trust and command attention without force is a leader's greatest strength.

As you move forward, remember that your leadership presence is crafted not only by what you say but by how you breathe, pause, and engage. Each silent moment and every measured breath become a building block in the architecture of trust and influence. By practising these subtle skills, you are not just leading—you are guiding with intention, inspiring with authenticity, and cultivating resilience within your teams. Master these nuances, and you will find that influence is not seized but naturally extended to those who lead with presence and poise.

PART TWO SUMMARY

The most important thing in communication is hearing what isn't said
Peter Drucker

Leadership is often thought of as verbal persuasion—the power of eloquent words and compelling arguments. However, beneath every great leader's voice lies a subtler, more profound layer of influence: non-verbal communication. Part Two, *Micro-Skills for Leaders*, illuminates this silent yet powerful domain, showing how gestures, tone, posture, and even breathing shape perceptions, foster emotional and psychological safety, and deepen trust.

Non-verbal leadership is not a supplementary skill—it is the foundation upon which all effective communication is built. Our evolutionary heritage has hardwired us to react instinctively to non-verbal cues—faster than we process words[1]. Long before language, body language and vocal tone signalled danger, communicated intent, and fostered cooperation. Today, those same primal sensitivities still govern how we trust and follow others, even in boardrooms and meeting spaces. Leaders who fail to recognise this instinctual layer risk miscommunication and mistrust, while those who master it inspire confidence and unity.

At the heart of non-verbal leadership lies *congruence*—the alignment between what is said and how it is expressed[2]. When a leader's words and non-verbal cues are in harmony, their message resonates with authenticity and authority. Conversely, misalignment—like nervous fidgeting paired with confident words—creates discomfort and doubt, eroding trust. Effective leadership begins with self-awareness: recognising and refining these unconscious cues is essential to influencing others with credibility.

This part takes readers on a journey from understanding non-verbal basics to mastering nuanced leadership presence..

- **Chapter 4, *The Elusive Obvious*,** introduced the power of non-verbal cues, tracing their evolutionary roots and explaining how they silently shape interactions before words are spoken. It highlights how non-verbal communication is processed instinctively, influencing trust and perception.
- **Chapter 5, *Non-Verbal Acuity*,** deepens this understanding by offering practical tools to refine non-verbal communication. Frameworks such as the PACE Protocol and techniques like the "Break and Breathe" method teach leaders how subtle adjustments in posture, eye contact, and tone can transform their presence and guide team dynamics.
- **Chapter 6, *The Subtle Skillset*,** explored advanced strategies—like the power of the pause, breath control, and third-point communication—that allow leaders to maintain authority and empathy even in high-pressure scenarios. Case stories, such as Karen's negotiation success and Angus's failed presentation, illustrate how non-verbal

mastery can either strengthen or undermine leadership outcomes.

Non-verbal leadership is not just about making a good impression—it is about creating an environment of trust, safety and resilience. By mastering the silent language of leadership, you can amplify your impact, foster deeper connections, and guide your team with both authority and empathy. These subtle skills are the cornerstone of building high-performing teams that can thrive in complexity and adapt to change.

Techniques Introduced in Part Two

1. **Non-Verbal Congruence**[3]: Aligning verbal and non-verbal cues for highest impact.
2. **Posture Awareness**[4]: Using open, upright posture to convey confidence.
3. **Eye Contact**[5]: Building trust and attentiveness through direct gaze.
4. **Tone Modulation**[6]: Controlling vocal tone to convey authority or approachability.
5. **The Power of the Pause**[7]: Using silence to create thoughtfulness and authority.
6. **Breath & Perception**[8]: Understanding how high/ low breathing affects how you are perceived
7. **BLIP**[9]: Using deep breathing to project calm and co-regulate group emotions.
8. **Peripheral Awareness**[10]: Sensing audience reactions without direct observation.
9. **Points of Focus**[11]: Shifting between inward focus, direct engagement, task-oriented focus, and conceptual vision.
10. **Non-Verbal Behavioural Clusters**[12]: Switching and blending *approachable* and *credible* patterns based on context.

11. **Eye-Hand Coordination**[13]: Guiding attention with synchronised gestures and gaze.
12. **How Not to Get Shot**[14]: Arranging non-verbals to minimise emotional discussions.
13. **Above (Pause) Whisper**[15]: A sequence for gaining and maintaining attention.

PART THREE
NARRATIVE & UNITY SKILLS

INTRODUCTION

I suggest that the story of the last few years strongly indicates that human action is nonlinear, that time and place matter a great deal[1]
Ralph Stacey

Leadership in times of transition tests the very limits of influence. As explored in Part Two, *Micro-Skills for Leaders*, influencers must master the silent language of gestures, tone, and presence to shape group dynamics and create safety. Yet, non-verbal communication alone cannot guide people through the complexities of change. To move teams from paralysis to progress, leaders must voice what has gone unspoken. They must *craft stories* that bridge the gap between instinctive trust and purposeful action, turning ambiguity into clarity and fear into hope.

Part Three, *Narrative & Unity Skills*, introduces the art and science of using narrative as a leadership tool in complexity. It builds on the non-verbal foundation of Part Two by adding words into the mix— not just any words, but those deliberately chosen to transform how people think, feel, and act.

Stories as Anchors in Chaos

Stories hold a unique power in leadership because they operate on two levels. First, they help us make sense of **objective reality**, providing coherence in a world that is often chaotic, ambiguous, and uncertain. This is where the work of Ralph Stacey, Dave Snowden, and Meg Wheatley becomes invaluable. In complex systems, where cause and effect are unclear, stories reveal patterns, uncover tacit knowledge, and foster shared understanding. As Snowden's *Cynefin* framework teaches, storytelling becomes a vital sense-making tool in environments where traditional logic falters[2].

Second, stories shape **subjective experience**. They do not merely describe reality; they transform how people perceive it. Drawing on insights from Stephen Porges' *Polyvagal Theory*[3] and Daniel Kahneman's work on cognitive biases, storytelling taps into the instincts and emotions that govern human behaviour. A well-told story can reframe adversity as opportunity, align people's emotional states with a shared vision, and inspire action even in the face of uncertainty.

Bridges of Belief

Change is the crucible of leadership. Transitions—whether they involve uniting disunited teams, navigating crises, or inspiring bold ventures—amplify disconnection, mistrust, and fear. In such moments, logic and directives alone are insufficient. Leaders must connect with the human experience of those they lead, weaving narratives that validate emotions, foster safety and align diverse perspectives.

In the quote above, Ralph Stacey reminds us that human action is nonlinear and deeply influenced by context. Leaders cannot impose order on complexity, but they can guide people through it by crafting stories that resonate. These narratives act as bridges, linking individual roles to a collective mission and transforming isolated efforts into cohesive action.

Consider the fractured dynamics of a team divided by silos, mistrust or resistance to change. A leader employing narrative framing does not merely communicate operational goals—they tell a story that illuminates the "why" behind the mission. The story transforms individual contributions into indispensable pieces of a greater whole, fostering trust, empathy and shared purpose.

A Framework for Influence

PACE Storytelling provides leaders with a structured approach to crafting and delivering these transformative narratives. Rooted in insights from complexity theory, neuroscience, and Richard Bandler's human change technologies[4], the framework bridges the gap between sense-making and meaning-making. It equips leaders to navigate two critical tasks:

1. **Sense-Making**: Revealing the hidden dynamics of complexity, helping teams understand their context and navigate ambiguity.
2. **Meaning-Making**: Shaping how people interpret their circumstances, enabling them to reframe challenges, align with shared values, and act with purpose.

By addressing both the objective and subjective dimensions of human experience, PACE Storytelling transforms leadership into an art of influence and alignment. It is designed to resonate across the three levels of the human mind:

- **Instinctual (Reptilian Brain)**: Engaging survival instincts through high-stakes risks and vivid imagery[5].
- **Emotional (Mammalian Brain)**: Fostering connection, trust, and empathy through shared experiences.
- **Rational (Primate Brain)**: Providing logic, vision, and intellectual stimulation to guide decision-making.

Story Structures for Transitions

Stories become indispensable during transitions, which are often fraught with fragmentation and paralysis. Whether leading a team fractured by silos, navigating a crisis that threatens morale, or inspiring a stagnant group to embrace bold change, leaders must tell stories that address their teams' instinctual, emotional, and rational needs.

For example, in moments of disunity, stories can bring people together by reframing divisions as opportunities for collaboration. During times of despair, stories can inspire hope by positioning adversity as the beginning of a shared journey toward renewal. And when teams are too comfortable to change, stories can spark the imagination, showing them a future worth striving for.

The stakes for leaders in these moments are high. Without effective narratives, they risk being perceived as irrelevant, obstructive, or even threatening. But when leaders succeed, the rewards are profound: they create environments where individuals feel safe, valued, and empowered to act.

A Preview of What Lies Ahead

The chapters in this part equip leaders to craft narratives that meet the demands of three iconic leadership transitions:

Chapter 7: Of Sense & Meaning focuses on the dual power of storytelling as both a sense-making and meaning-making tool. Leaders learn to unify teams and foster resilience through narratives that engage instinct, emotion, and intellect. By framing reality, building shared understanding, and inspiring collective purpose, this chapter demonstrates how storytelling provides clarity amidst complexity. It introduces the evolved PACE framework and examines practical applications of sense-making through Dave Snowden's insights and meaning-making through Richard Bandler's transformative approaches.

Chapter 8: "Band of Brothers" explores the unifying power of storytelling during challenging transitions. Using the *Unity BRIDGE* framework, leaders discover how to dismantle silos, align diverse groups around shared values, and establish psychological safety. The chapter highlights how storytelling can transform fractured teams into cohesive, resilient units, with real-world examples that illustrate its fractal application across organisational scales.

Chapter 9: "Les Misérables" delves into how leaders can guide teams through moments of despair to renewal and growth. Drawing lessons from historical figures like Nelson Mandela, Mahatma Gandhi, and Abraham Lincoln, the chapter highlights the power of narrative to rebuild trust, align values, and inspire resilience. It introduces the *FOCUS UP* framework, offering leaders tools to transform crises into opportunities for collective progress, uniting teams with compassion, clarity, and purpose.

These chapters provide leaders with actionable tools to influence group dynamics, rebuild trust, and inspire transformation. By mastering the art of storytelling, leaders can create neuro-resilient organisations that thrive in complexity, uniting their teams under shared values and a common vision.

The Leadership Narrative Challenge

Unlike world leaders with teams of strategists and speechwriters, most organisational leaders must rely on their instincts, experience, and resolve to guide teams through uncertainty. They are the mid-level managers, CEOs of small nonprofits, and owners of struggling family businesses who bear the weight of these responsibilities alone. This part is written for *them*, offering practical, actionable frameworks to help them craft stories that inspire, unite, and move their teams forward.

Leadership begins with what is unsaid, but it is the words leaders choose—woven into compelling narratives—that turn silence into strength and complexity into opportunity. As we delve into *PACE Storytelling*, consider the stories you want to tell. What will you say to shape the future of your teams, organisations, and communities?

SEVEN
OF SENSE & MEANING

*The most powerful person in the world is the storyteller.
The storyteller sets the vision, values,
and agenda of an entire generation that is to come.*
Steve Jobs

STORYTELLING IS A PRIMARY SKILL — it is not something to be added once the 'real' leadership work is done. History and neuroscience confirm this. The leaders who shaped history were those who shaped the stories that defined it.

The Steve Jobs quote above encapsulates the timeless influence of storytelling. In a world filled with complexity and uncertainty, leaders who can craft and share compelling narratives possess a unique power: the ability to connect, align, and inspire.

Consider a ship navigating turbulent seas. Without a unifying story to guide its crew—a narrative compass to bring purpose and direction—they risk drifting aimlessly, consumed by confusion and distrust.

Conversely, a shared story transforms a fragmented group into a cohesive team, resilient and focused on reaching their destination. This is the transformative power of storytelling.

For leaders, storytelling is more than an art—it is a necessity. It bridges the gaps between chaos and clarity, sense-making, meaning-making, teaching and individual growth and collective purpose. It is not just a tool for communication but a means of fostering meaning and unity.

This chapter explores why stories matter, how they enable sense-making and meaning-making, and how leaders can use frameworks like PACE to inspire and sustain their teams. Leadership, at its core, is *storytelling*.

Why Stories Matter

Since the first humans, stories have been our most enduring tool for survival, understanding and sharing knowledge. From ancient cave paintings to futuristic digital media, stories have shaped our understanding of the world, our place within it, and our relationships with others. Stories are far more than entertainment; they are blueprints for survival, teaching us lessons, values, and shared purpose.

Consider a small group of early humans huddled around a fire. One recounts a successful hunt—where to find prey, which dangers to avoid, and the strategies that led to triumph. In that moment, the storyteller is not just sharing an event but transferring knowledge, building connection, and fostering confidence. Thousands of years later, though the contexts have changed, the essence of storytelling remains the same: it binds people together, passes down wisdom and mobilises collective action.

Stories engage the human mind in ways facts and data alone cannot. Stories have an extraordinary ability to touch the deepest recesses of our minds, engaging not just our cognition but also our emotions and instincts. Stories arouse all three of the Reptilian Brain, Mammalian Brain and Primate Brain, captivating us in ways that transcend facts and data.

The Reptilian Brain responds to stories which contain high stakes risks. A tale of survival, with its vivid descriptions of peril and triumph, grips this part of the brain. Think of a story where a character narrowly escapes a predator or endures an unrelenting storm. Our Reptilian Brain reacts as though the events were happening to us, "right here, right now". It sharpens our focus, heightens our awareness, and sets our bodies on edge, ready for action.

The Mammalian Brain operates as the centre of our emotional life. This brain thrives on connection and compassion, finding resonance in stories of love, loss, friendship and community. When a story portrays a parent sacrificing for their child or friends overcoming adversity together, this brain floods us with emotions. These narratives release oxytocin, deepening our sense of trust and attachment. A well-told story does more than entertain; it builds bridges between the teller and the listener, creating a shared emotional reality.

The Primate Brain is humanity's evolutionary crowning achievement, the realm of abstract thought, logic, and imagination. The Primate Brain loves puzzles, thrives on moral dilemmas, and savours complex ideas. It delights in stories that challenge conventional wisdom or offer intellectual surprises. Consider a plot twist that recontextualises the entire narrative or a philosophical parable that forces us to question long-held beliefs. Such stories invite reflection, spurring us to connect the dots, consider alternatives, and perhaps even change our worldview.

A well-told story weaves together instincts, emotions, and intellect, creating a seamless thread that speaks to the gut, heart and head alike. A masterful narrative works by weaving together survival stakes, emotional resonance, and intellectual depth into a rapture of engagement.

Think of the classic hero's journey: the protagonist faces life-threatening danger (Reptilian Brain), wrestles with emotional challenges and relationships (Mammalian Brain), and ultimately achieves a transformative insight or victory that carries profound meaning (Primate Brain). It is no wonder that such stories endure across cultures and generations—they speak to the entirety of our humanity.

This interplay of brains also explains why stories are evolutionarily effective. For the Reptilian Brain, they act as simulations, preparing us for real-world risks and opportunities. For the Mammalian Brain, they provide a shared emotional language that strengthens social cohesion. And for the Primate Brain, they encode complex knowledge in a form that is both memorable and compelling. In this way, stories are not just thrilling; they are tools of survival, connection, adaption and resilience. For leaders, these characteristics of storytelling hold a transformative power.

A leader who understands how stories engage instincts is not at the mercy of group emotions but can guide them. By shaping narratives that resonate with all three levels of cognition, leaders move teams from reactivity to resilience.

Consider Nelson Mandela, who united a fractured nation not through statistics or policy details but by framing a narrative of hope, justice and shared destiny. His story inspired belief and action, demonstrating that stories do not just communicate—they galvanise.

During times of uncertainty, stories become even more essential. They provide clarity and direction, helping teams navigate ambiguity and align around a shared vision. Without a guiding story, anxiety spreads and disunity takes hold. But with one, leaders can foster resilience, purpose, and progress.

Stories matter because they connect us to each other, shape how we see the world, and inspire us to move forward together. To lead, the leader must tell stories that matter to the people they lead.

THE SENSE-MAKER

Dave Snowden, a leading thinker in complexity science, helps people and organisations grapple with the volatility, ambiguity and uncertainty that define complexity. He has developed an array of ways to glimpse into complexity to get some inkling into what is really going on. Snowden is a true *sense-maker*.

Sense-making is the process of creating coherence from chaos, a vital skill in leadership. In today's fast-changing environments, leaders often face ambiguity and complexity that challenge even the most robust plans. Here, storytelling emerges as a powerful tool—not just for explaining complexity, but for navigating and transforming it into shared understanding.

At its core, sense-making connects disparate observations into a unified narrative, aligning individuals toward a common purpose. Dave Snowden highlights storytelling's role in this process. In his *Cynefin Framework*, Snowden argues that in complex systems, cause and effect are not always clear. Leaders must instead use tools like *Anecdote Circles* (augmented in Chapter 2 into PACE Strengths and PACE Surfacing), which gather micro-narratives—short, lived experiences—to reveal patterns within the system.

Consider a manufacturing company transitioning to semi-automation. Tensions between shop floor workers and management escalate, and productivity plummets. Instead of imposing a top-down solution, leaders facilitate small-group discussions to capture employee narratives. Workers share concerns about job security, pride in craftsmanship, and frustrations over exclusion from decision-making. These narratives, collected through *Anecdote Circles*, reveal underlying emotional dynamics: resistance is not rooted in opposition to automation but in a lack of trust and a low sense of agency.

Using these insights, leaders craft a new narrative. This story acknowledges workers' fears, celebrates their expertise, and frames semi-automation as a collaborative effort to improve outcomes for everyone. The narrative transforms resistance into engagement, fostering trust and alignment.

Snowden's approach also incorporates *Safe-to-Fail Experiments*, small-scale interventions designed to explore solutions without fear of major repercussions. For example, the company might involve workers in co-designing workflows for semi-automation. By framing these experiments as part of a shared story—one where employees are active contributors rather than passive recipients—leaders create a sense of ownership and shared purpose.

It integrates logic and emotion, engaging both the Primate mind that seeks patterns and the emotional core that craves meaning. A purely rational explanation may satisfy the intellect but leave people disengaged. A compelling story, on the other hand, weaves facts and feelings into a relatable narrative that inspires action.

Sense-making through storytelling is particularly critical in complex systems where solutions are not linear. Leaders who embrace this approach can illuminate hidden dynamics, align diverse perspectives and guide their teams through uncertainty. As Snowden's work demonstrates, stories are not static—they are living tools that adapt and evolve with the challenges they address.

In the hands of a skilled leader, storytelling is the compass that turns ambiguity into shared understanding, enabling teams to navigate complexity with clarity and confidence.

The Meaning-Maker

Richard Bandler, co-creator of Neuro-Linguistic Programming (NLP), is a teacher. His teaching is more than just the transmission of information, although there is that aspect. Rather, his teaching is the art of transforming meaning and, in doing so, changes the way people think, feel and behave afterwards. Bandler is a true *meaning-maker*.

Stories, with their unique ability to inspire and engage, are the ultimate teaching tool. They connect with people on a deeper level, bypassing resistance and fostering new perspectives. Leaders who master storytelling as a teaching method can guide their teams to embrace change and grow beyond their limitations.

Richard Bandler recognised the transformative power of storytelling. Amongst the array of storytelling and linguistic tools that he has created, Bandler uses techniques like *reframing, nested loops,* and *heteromorphic metaphors* to help people see challenges differently and unlock new possibilities. For Bandler, stories are active agents of change, capable of bypassing conscious resistance and speaking directly to the unconscious mind.

Consider a leader addressing a team paralysed by fear of failure. Instead of delivering a lecture on resilience, the leader shares a personal story: how they faced rejection early in their career but reframed those setbacks as stepping stones. The story subtly plants a new perspective—failure is not an endpoint but part of a larger journey. Without explicit instruction, the team begins to see challenges as opportunities for growth.

Bandler's *nested loops* technique illustrates how storytelling can embed profound lessons. Picture a story within a story, each layer adding depth and nuance. For example, Bandler might recount a client overcoming anxiety by learning to reframe their fears, interwoven with a metaphor about a river carving its path through obstacles. Bandler engages all three levels of the triune brain to get the desired response from the listener.

As soon as he detects the response, without concluding the story, he switches the story in search of his next desired response. He closes the loops, by concluding the stories, in the reverse order from which they were originally told. It is a beautiful piece of highly effective meaning-making where the listener has internalised its message within each triune level, often without realising it.

Reframing is especially powerful in leadership and a critical leadership ability to reframe the narratives surfaced during the sense-making phase. A team that views obstacles as insurmountable will struggle to act. But when those same obstacles are framed as challenges to overcome, the team gains momentum and determination. For instance, a struggling organisation might be galvanised by a story of past crises where collective effort led to success. The leader's narrative does not deny current difficulties but places them within a broader arc of resilience and renewal.

Storytelling also fosters connection. When a leader shares a story, it humanises them, allowing the audience to see themselves in its characters and scenarios. This shared identification builds trust and empathy, essential foundations for any transformation to take root.

Meaning-making through storytelling is not a soft skill; it is the most effective way a leader can successfully engage with and influence the complex adaptive system of the Hive Mind. To paraphrase Bandler:

> By influencing the way that the Hive Mind thinks and feels, you influence the way it behaves

---

By crafting narratives that reframe perspectives and inspire new ways of thinking, leaders empower their teams to move beyond limitations.

They are not merely imparting knowledge, they transform its meaning across all three levels of the Triune Brain, creating a bridge to transform the group—one story at a time.

In leadership, meaning-making is about more than delivering solutions. It is about creating the conditions for growth, fostering group resilience, and inspiring belief in the groups own agency to alter their current circumstances—all through the timeless power of storytelling.

From Sense to *Meaning*

Superficially, sense-making and meaning-making might seem like separate processes. Sense-making focuses on interpreting ambiguity and uncovering tacit knowledge, while meaning-making reframes this knowledge into explicit insights that can inspire action. Yet, these two processes are deeply intertwined, forming an iterative cycle where each amplifies the other. Storytelling is the bridge that connects them: storytelling is both the input into and the output out of these combined processes. They enable leaders to move seamlessly between sense-discovery and the transformation of meaning.

Consider a river system as a metaphor. Sense-making is the network of tributaries collecting streams of tacit knowledge—anecdotes, emotions, and experiences—from the landscape. Meaning-making channels this raw material into a focused current, shaping it into Triune Brain understanding that provides direction. Without sense-making, meaning-making lacks depth and breadth. Without meaning-making, sense-making risks remaining diffuse and unfocused.

Without both, just like the proverbial butterfly whose flapping wings cause a tornado on the other side of the planet, organisations and societies can be subject to destructive positive feedback loops.

Think of the 'Arab Spring' which spread like a wildfire destabilising and toppling regimes across North Africa and the Middle East; or the spontaneous riots and attacks on illegal migrants across England because of three children being stabbed to death.

Consider a tech start-up grappling with market disruption. Through sense-making techniques, the leadership gathers micro-narratives from employees, uncovering fears of obsolescence, pride in innovation, and frustrations with unclear priorities. These insights reveal a fragmented organisation, but they also point toward hidden strengths. The leader then uses storytelling to reframe these narratives, weaving them into a story of resilience and adaptability that hits all parts of the Triune Brain. The new narrative aligns the team's understanding and inspires a shared commitment to innovate.

This iterative process underscores storytelling's dual role: it illuminates hidden dynamics while reframing them into actionable insights. Leaders skilled in storytelling can guide their teams through ambiguity by uncovering the group's unconscious patterns and aligning them with a collective vision.

By bridging sense-making and teaching, storytelling transforms complexity into clarity, fostering both understanding and action. In an era where adaptability is paramount, mastering this dynamic is essential for leaders seeking to inspire, align, and sustain their teams.

THE PACE STORYTELLING MODEL

The *PACE framework* has already demonstrated its versatility in this book. Its applications evolving through multiple repurposing to meet the demands of different leadership challenges.

Introduced in Chapter Two, the PACE Protocol *was designed as a tool to help coaches and practitioners track their progress during safety rupture repair and coaching sessions.* Of course, the client was oblivious to the phases through which they were being transitioned. However, the protocol served as a *straightforward 'outer game' map and compass*, allowing practitioners to keep oriented and on track as they move sequentially through the rupture repair process.

PACE functions like a *flight navigation system*, guiding leaders and coaches through a structured sequence where each phase builds on the last.

1. *Set the foundation* – Establish initial safety conditions, ensuring readiness to engage by probing for permission.
2. *Navigate the journey* – Address the key objectives of the current phase, ensuring progress and alignment.
3. *Clear for transition* – Once the criteria for the current phase are met, transition naturally into the next stage.
4. *Land and integrate* – When the final phase is complete, exit the structured process, allowing the new insights and strategies to take root.

This sequential approach provided clarity and structure, helping coaches teach their clients about their own 'inner game', training them how to repair their own safety ruptures. That is, by the end of the session, the client walks away with a set of new understanding and ways of thinking, with which to sustain their socially connected state: in simple terms, they learn how to 'feel safe from the skin in'.

Later, in Chapter Three, PACE was adapted for 'inner game' support for *leader autoregulation and event prep*, empowering leaders to stabilise their internal states before 'outer game' engagements.

In Chapter Two, Dave Snowden's *Anecdote Circles* idea was augmented into PACE *Strengths*, which had the narrow focus of strength-led conversations, to surface tacit knowledge and latent narratives towards improving at the local level.

In the second, PACE *Surfacing*, had no topic of focus. It sought to uncover raw emergent narratives, from many and varied sources.

Each occasion a narrative is recorded, it is treated as a data point. These data are analysed, grouped into types, clusters and patterns, from which inferences can be drawn, and distributed throughout the organisation.

While all these earlier versions were guided through an imperceptible phased process, they were worked because their application was in constrained environments, such as small group conversations, with specific goal criteria: achieve 1) safety and permission, 2) 'inner game' control, 3) 'outer game' sociability and 5) new learnings and understanding. In addition, the leader, coach or facilitator was present throughout and would respond to the vicissitudes of these conversations, guiding participants through to a conclusion.

In short, it was a 'closed system': a straightforward, time-bound process with a consciously chosen end goal.

However, the leadership function of 'narrative framing' is not about surfacing emergent narratives. It is about reframing those narrative data-points towards a useful way of thinking about what is happening and, by proliferating that new frame, influence the beliefs and behaviours of the Hive Mind.

Of course, this is easier said than done. The Hive Mind is not a closed system, it is an open one. It is not straightforward, it is complex. It is not of short duration, it is an ongoing long-term entity. It does not have a specific consciously chosen goal, it has multiple conscious and unconscious, overt and covert, interests and agendas. Some of these are mutually compatible, some incompatible; and some are cooperative and competitive.

In environments of *volatility, uncertainty and ambiguity*, leaders face multiple points of instability. These points of instability are due, in part, because of the complex and adapting dynamics of their system (Hive Mind) within which they are operating. They are also due to how this system responds to the larger external complex and adapting system, in which their system is a participant.

Exhausted leaders find themselves constantly tackling sporadic, plural and diverse problems. Their traditional linear management methodologies fail to get control over the nonlinear dynamics, both within and from without, the system in which they lead. The Hive Mind does not respond to top-down logic alone but requires a story compelling enough to override its internal contradictions. To navigate these challenges, the PACE framework was modified to address the iterative, concurrent, and responsive needs of *complex adaptive systems*.

The PACE Storytelling Framework

At its core, *PACE Storytelling* helps leaders navigate complexity by addressing both the socio-psychological and behavioural dimensions of group dynamics. It provides four key points of ongoing focus that guide the crafting and delivery of stories:

1. *Permission:* Leadership storytelling begins with establishing group safety. By creating an environment where people feel heard and valued, leaders gain implicit permission to influence. This step ensures that the audience is receptive and engaged, setting the stage for deeper connections.
2. *Agency:* Narratives must empower groups to rise above instinctual reactions, such as fear or defensiveness, in order to enable collective, thoughtful responses. 'Leadership credibility' as expressed in their verbal and non-verbal cues, as well as their cognitive reasoning and action, is an important variable.

Framing challenges as opportunities is only believable if it is delivered by leaders who are perceived to be grounded, credible and intelligent.

Such leaders are able to guide their teams to act with intentionality rather than impulsivity.

3. *Connection:* Effective narrative framing fosters unity and alignment by creating shared meaning and group cohesion. Narratives should resonate with collective values and goals, transforming a diverse group into a unified team with a common purpose; or a distressed group towards somewhere better.
4. *Embedding:* The ultimate goal is to influence thoughts, feelings, and behaviours of the Hive Mind in a way that builds flexibility and resilience. By embedding new meanings into the group's narrative, leaders can foster adaptability, innovation, and sustained progress in the face of complexity.

Phase Shift

In its *narrative framing* form, the prior 'phases', each with its own goal/ exit criteria, become *Unity-Stabilising Inputs* (USIs). Once initiated, like the Hive Mind, the USIs are ongoing and have no exit criteria. Rather, they have operating criteria, which are monitored and sustained through leadership interventions.

USIs are not phases to complete but *rhythms to maintain*—like spinning plates, each element requires continuous attention during and after their roll out:

1. *Start the first stabiliser* – Establish psychological safety as the first key input and ensure it remains steady as permission is secured.
2. *Expand stability* – Introduce additional stabilisers while maintaining those already in motion.
3. *Sustain the balance* – Adapt to shifting conditions, reinforcing alignment as needed.
4. *Intervene as required* – Leadership is a constant act of recalibration; respond proactively to instability before it cascades.

THIS ADAPTATION TURNS the PACE Protocol into a flexible framework that supports group resilience. Much like a juggler in a 'spinning plates' routine, leaders must ensure that each USI—once initiated—remains stable and responsive to the group's shifting needs. This monitoring often combines *hard metrics* (e.g., KPIs) with *soft metrics* (e.g., trust surveys or anecdotal insights), ensuring that narratives remain grounded in the group's lived experiences.

Importantly, these performance indicators will be *indicative*, not definitive: they are proxies for what is really happening. As such, these indicators themselves should be subject to revision. Whilst such metrics are often omitted, they should form part of an AAR in the aftermath of a 'surprise'. Because misplaced trust and confidence in nondefinitive KPIs can erode quickly and strip leadership of its perceived credibility.

As Mark Twain put it:

> "It ain't what you don't know that gets you into trouble. It's what you know for sure that just ain't so".

Or, as my colleague, Michael Grinder, says:

> 'Surprise is the enemy of competence'.

The importance of sensitive and reliable performance indicators is important, for example:

- How do you know exactly whether you have broad-based permission for a strategic initiative?
  - If you are operating under that assumption falsely, the success of your initiatives will be compromised.
  - In the event of failure, you may be convinced that it was the project's execution that was at fault.
  - But it might well have been the Hive Mind's willingness to adopt the initiative that was the issue.

STORYTELLING for Resilience

Through this evolution, the *PACE Storytelling framework* transforms leadership narratives into adaptive, *living frameworks*. Drawing on *Polyvagal Theory* and *Neuro-Linguistic Programming* (NLP), PACE addresses group safety, autonomy, cohesion, and resilience as ongoing processes. Among its many strengths, it equips leaders to:

1. Take disunited and estranged groups and unite them.

2. Guide teams from challenging circumstances to better outcomes.

The result is more than effective communication; it is the creation of a *neuro-resilient group dynamic*, where individuals and teams alike thrive in the face of complexity. By evolving from a protocol into the iterative flexibility of USI frameworks, PACE ensures that leadership storytelling becomes the foundation for *growth, adaptability and long-term success.*

Leaders who influence effectively do not simply tell a story once and expect it to hold. They tend to it, reinforce it, evolve it. Unity-Stabilising Inputs (USIs) allow leaders to maintain the delicate balance between reinforcing a shared reality and adapting to new challenges.

USI Frameworks

PACE Storytelling is a very useful generic framework is a quick and easy go to and can suit small to medium organisations well. It's easy to understand, teach and review. In addition, over the years, I have developed other USI frameworks, many of which do not fall within the PACE structure. However, I would like to introduce you to two which were derived from PACE and each refined to better suit two specific leadership contexts.

- *'Unity BRIDGE'* focuses on uniting disparate groups, such as merging teams or diverse stakeholders, by emphasising shared values and goals.
- *'FOCUS UP'* guides leaders in moving teams from adversity to progress by framing challenges as stepping stones toward a brighter future.

These frameworks maintain PACE's iterative nature, ensuring that narratives evolve alongside the group's needs.

The next two chapters are dedicated to exploring these two frameworks in depth. By examining Unity BRIDGE and FOCUS UP, leaders will gain practical tools to stabilise group cohesion, foster trust, and guide their teams through the complexities of current challenges.

Key Takeaways

The PACE framework transforms storytelling from an abstract concept into a structured, actionable leadership tool. By addressing safety, agency, connection, and resilience, it equips leaders with a narrative compass that fosters trust and alignment. Whether uniting fractured teams or navigating crises, PACE extends beyond communication to create resilient group dynamics.

Two derivative frameworks, Unity BRIDGE and FOCUS UP, were developed to enable leaders to craft living narratives that evolve with their teams. In complex systems where uncertainty prevails, PACE-style frameworks empower leaders to transform ambiguity into progress, inspiring sustainable growth and shared purpose.

STORYTELLING IS NOT an ornament of leadership; it is its essence. A well-told story does more than transmit information—it reorganises perception, reshapes belief, and reorients action. It transforms disorder into clarity, doubt into resolve, and disunity into shared direction. It is, in every meaningful sense, the bridge between complexity and understanding.

Steve Jobs once claimed that the storyteller is the most powerful person in the world, setting the vision, values, and agenda for the future. He was not speaking metaphorically. Every major shift in history—every great movement, every profound transformation—has been preceded by a story that reframed reality.

The Enlightenment did not begin with a set of policies but with a shift in narrative about reason, liberty, and human potential. The Civil Rights Movement gained momentum not through statistics but through stories that made injustice visceral, undeniable, and urgent. Leadership, at its core, is the craft of narrative shaping.

Yet, storytelling in leadership is not mere rhetoric—it is a structural necessity. A leader without a story is a ship without a compass, drifting at the mercy of external forces. Teams without unifying narratives fragment under pressure. Organisations without compelling stories fail to cohere, leaving individuals navigating uncertainty alone. A well-structured story is not just a means of making sense of the present but an invitation to participate in a shared future.

This chapter has explored the two intertwined dimensions of narrative: sense-making and meaning-making. Sense-making, as Dave Snowden argues, is how we detect patterns within complexity, gathering micro-narratives and surfacing implicit tensions before they become fault lines. Meaning-making, as Richard Bandler demonstrates, is the art of reframing those patterns, embedding new significance into familiar experiences, and unlocking fresh pathways for action. The most skilled leaders oscillate between these two processes, using stories to reveal, reframe, and realign.

The PACE framework, introduced in earlier chapters, provides a structured approach to this process. First, a leader must 'prime and probe', creating the psychological safety necessary for narratives to take hold. Without this, even the most compelling story will be met with resistance. Second, they must empower agency over instinct, ensuring that storytelling does not merely evoke emotion but mobilises action. Third, they must connect and socialise, crafting narratives that bind individuals into a collective, making the story a lived experience rather than an abstract ideal. Finally, they must embed strategies and meanings, ensuring that narratives are not fleeting moments of inspiration but enduring, adaptive frameworks for resilience.

A static story dies. A living story evolves. The next chapters will explore how frameworks like Unity BRIDGE and FOCUS UP extend these principles, providing structured tools for leaders to forge shared identities and mobilise teams through adversity. These are not theoretical exercises; they are essential practices for leading in a world where uncertainty is not an exception but the rule.

So, the question is not whether you will tell stories. You already do. The question is whether you will tell them consciously, with precision and purpose, shaping the minds, emotions, and instincts of those you lead. In a world brimming with competing narratives, only those who master the craft of storytelling will have the power to set the direction for what comes next.

What story will you tell? And who will follow you because of it?

EIGHT
"BAND OF BROTHERS"

We few, we happy few, we band of brothers[1]
William Shakespeare

'*BAND OF BROTHERS* was never just a book. It was a truth plainly told—of what happens when people, not joined by blood but by purpose, forge a bond tougher than circumstance. The title of this chapter is no mere homage. It's a directive. A quiet echo of *Henry V*, yes—but more than that, a signal. Great leadership doesn't just organise—it unites. It doesn't manage noise; it draws out harmony. Brotherhood of this kind isn't handed down by rank or role. It's forged in shared strain, earned in risk, and sealed by the unspoken decision to hold the line together. That's when a group becomes more than a collection of individuals. That's when it becomes one.

Have you ever walked into a new workplace where half the faces are unfamiliar, where old alliances linger, and where the future feels uncertain? How does a leader turn that loose collection of individuals, cliques and uncertainty into unity? Snowden's insight reminds us that narrative is not just how we communicate—it's how we cohere. It is the thread binding individuals into a collective, the bridge between unfamiliarity and shared purpose.

Bringing people together is not enough. Co-location does not create collaboration. A leader's true challenge is not in moving bodies into the same space, but in weaving a shared identity. Take, for instance, the opening of a new distribution centre (DC), a transition that reveals the full complexity of unity in motion.

Indeed, this transition story is about a large-scale *consolidation* involving the closure of four previous sites, a significant reorganisation of roles, and a mix of voluntary and involuntary redundancies. It's a period marked by profound change and, naturally, a mix of apprehension and optimism among team members.

The workforce now encompasses individuals from various levels—shop floor workers, supervisors, administrative staff, and management—each bringing different experiences and expectations. And as they come together, the need to forge a unified identity is crucial. Without this unity, the new DC would struggle to establish the foundation it needs to thrive.

Much like the Hive Mind discussed in Chapter 1, an organisation's strength lies not only in its individual components but in the ability of these components to operate harmoniously as one. However, unity doesn't simply materialise from co-location or organisational mandates. Instead, it's cultivated, nurtured and strengthened through deliberate efforts to break down barriers, rally around shared values, and establish a common purpose. This is where the *Unity BRIDGE* framework comes into play.

True unity isn't about removing differences—it's about synchronising them. A great orchestra does not demand that every instrument play the same note; it demands that each musician contributes to the whole. The Unity BRIDGE framework operates on the same principle: it transforms individual differences into collective strength, aligning diverse perspectives into a single, dynamic force.

Each *'Unity Stabilising Input'* (USI) of the framework supports the overall goal of creating a single, resilient entity out of many subgroups or factions. Through this framework, the new DC team will transition from disparate groups to a unified force, bringing out the best in each member and fostering a truly collaborative environment. While narrative shapes the collective identity of a workforce, the patterns of interaction within that workforce also play a critical role in maintaining unity.

FRACTAL Structure

> *I see fractals in the turbulence of human life*
> *each action may seem independent,*
> *but they are part of a larger self-organizing system*
> **Benoit Mandelbrot**

In Chapter 1, we explored collective intelligence as an emergent phenomenon, often seen in complex adaptive systems. Mandelbrot's observation reminds us that what appear to be isolated actions—decisions, conversations or team efforts—are in fact interconnected, shaping and being shaped by the larger dynamics of the system. This principle holds true in organisations, where even small acts or statements can ripple across teams, influencing morale, communication, and performance.

In a distribution centre, for example, a single decision about scheduling can cascade through the system, amplifying trust or sparking friction depending on how it is perceived. This interconnectedness is characteristic of what Meg Wheatley calls *'living systems'*, which we see in nature—storm formations, locust swarms or starling murmurations. These systems exhibit repeating patterns at different scales, providing stability while remaining adaptable.

Leadership is not about grand pronouncements; it is about repeated patterns of connection. The strength of an organisation, much like a fractal, is found in the symmetry between small moments and large outcomes. A single act of trust—one recalibration, one alignment—creates ripples that reorganise the entire system. These Unity Stabilising Inputs (USIs) provide leaders with tools to influence the system both broadly and in specific situations, from strategic initiatives to team meetings.

These *negative feedback loop*s are like a built-in self-correction system. Think of it as your car's cruise control. When the car goes too fast, the system automatically slows it down; when it's too slow, it speeds it up. This keeps the car at a steady speed.

In organisations, negative feedback loops work the same way. They help maintain balance by automatically adjusting to keep things on track. For example, if trust between teams starts to drop, a good leader might notice the signs—like miscommunication or tension—and take action to rebuild trust before it causes bigger problems.

It's called "negative" not because it's bad, but because it reduces or counters something that's going off-course—like slowing a car that's speeding or stopping a team conflict before it escalates. These loops help organisations adapt and stay stable in changing environments.

Like the repeating patterns of fern leaves at large and small scales, the framework ensures consistency and coherence across all communication levels, creating alignment even in dynamic and unpredictable environments. Leaders are not simply following sequential steps; they are managing multiple elements simultaneously, addressing emerging challenges to maintain equilibrium.

For example, if communication breaks down between shop floor workers and supervisors, it may destabilise other areas like trust or collaboration. Leaders must act swiftly to restore alignment, much like a juggler doing a spinning plates routine will stabilise a plate that is beginning to wobble. This iterative, non-linear approach enables leaders to keep the system cohesive while adapting to real-time conditions.

By understanding the fractal nature of organisations, leaders can better anticipate ripple effects and intervene effectively. This framework not only helps establish initial alignment but ensures that this alignment persists through the inevitable turbulence of a living system.

Snowden's narrative insights and Mandelbrot's fractal patterns equip leaders with practical tools to achieve unity in complex organisations. Together, they form the backbone of the Unity BRIDGE framework.

Unity BRIDGE Framework

USI 1: **B**reak Down Barriers

The first endeavour towards creating unity within any organisation, especially one as large and complex as a consolidated distribution centre (DC), is to address and dismantle the barriers that naturally arise between different groups and roles. Picture a landscape divided by fences and gates, each segment occupied by teams that have developed their own ways of doing things, honed by years of familiarity. These 'territories' serve a purpose—they define roles and responsibilities. But they also breed suspicion, limit collaboration, and create a fragmented organisational culture.

In our DC example, the individuals from the four closed sites bring with them different work practices, habits and often an ingrained sense of loyalty to their former teams. Each group has its unique history, shared experiences, and perhaps even internal jargon or shorthand that feels foreign to others.

Now, imagine these groups coming together under one roof. It's like asking players from different sports to form a single team. While they may all be 'athletes', their training, language and approaches differ. To succeed as a team, they must learn each other's strengths, respect each other's perspectives, and adopt a shared way of working.

Cross-Functional Interaction

The practical approach to breaking down these barriers begins with creating opportunities for meaningful interaction. This isn't just about placing people from different teams at the same table; it's about designing situations that require real collaboration. Cross-departmental projects and collaborative training sessions are essential first steps.

For instance, as the DC team adapts to new semi-automated processes, a training programme that includes shop floor workers, supervisors, admin staff, and management can facilitate shared learning. Not only does this approach break down practical knowledge silos, but it also builds mutual understanding as each group gains insights into the other's contributions and challenges.

Additionally, open forums and structured dialogues can create safe places where team members can voice their thoughts without fear of judgement. Leaders must encourage transparency and demonstrate that they are receptive to input. When team members across roles see that their insights are not only heard but also respected, trust begins to grow organically. In this way, the psychological fences start to come down, making it harder for an 'us vs. them' mentality to persist.

Key Insight: Breaking down barriers is about more than erasing physical or logistical divides; it's about dismantling the psychological walls that often isolate groups within organisa-

tions. With that in mind, humans form cliques all the time. With respect to the 'plate-spinning' point, leaders need to be alert to the return of old cliques, as well as the spontaneous emergence of new ones.

For the new DC team, this means moving beyond individual roles and creating a shared culture where everyone's perspectives are valued. Unity begins to flourish when team members see each other's contributions as essential.

USI 2: Rally Around Shared Values

Once the physical and psychological barriers begin to dissolve, the next step is to rally the team around shared values. Shared values act as the unifying core of an organisation, providing a collective foundation that goes beyond job titles or functional roles.

Consider shared values as the roots of a large tree; while the branches may spread in different directions, each branch draws nourishment from the same source. In organisations, values like respect, resilience, and quality serve this function, uniting diverse individuals under a common purpose.

In the case of the DC, rallying around shared values is especially important. The team includes people who have had very different experiences, not only in terms of job roles but also in terms of workplace culture.

For example, shop floor workers may have priorities that differ significantly from those of administrative staff, just as supervisors may have different viewpoints compared to senior management. However, by focusing on shared values, we can transcend these differences.

. . .

Building a New Culture

For the DC, core values such as *Respect, Resilience,* and *Quality* provided a guiding framework. Respect ensures that every member—regardless of role—feels valued and acknowledged for their contributions. Resilience emphasises the importance of supporting each other through the transition, recognising that each person is adapting to new systems, environments, and expectations.

Commitment to quality unites the team around a shared goal of excellence in everything they do, from logistical efficiency on the shop floor to meticulous data management in admin roles. Leaders can actively reinforce these values through regular "values-alignment" sessions, where team members from different roles discuss how these values translate into their specific tasks.

For example, during a session focused on quality, a shop floor worker might share how their attention to detail in packing ensures accuracy, while an admin staff member could explain how timely data entry supports the entire chain of distribution. Such sessions enable the team to see how each role, in its unique way, upholds the organisation's values, fostering mutual appreciation.

Key Insight: *Shared values are more than aspirational statements; they are the glue that binds diverse teams together. Values, therefore, have to be manifested in all aspects of organisation life. With our plate-spinning analogy in mind, leaders need to be vigilant for any degrading of values in action. If respect, resilience and quality are no longer the lived values, some other values will be. Regardless of whether they are espoused in official documents, the lived values are those in operation.*

By rallying around these values, the new DC team can create a collective identity that bridges differences, reduces fragmentation, and enhances cooperation.

USI 3: **I**nspire with Vision

As barriers are coming down and shared values are becoming embedded throughout the organisation, inspiring the team with a convincing and compelling vision is the next 'plate to spin'. Extending the metaphor, if shared values are the roots of the tree, vision is the sunlight, drawing everyone upwards and guiding their collective endeavour and growth. A clear and resonating vision is essential, especially during times of transition, as it provides direction and instils a sense of purpose in each member.

Inspiring with vision, however, requires more than setting a direction; it demands communication that is both vivid and meaningful. Leaders must create the connective tissue between the abstract and the practical, making the vision feel personal and immediate.

Allan, the General Manager of the new DC, encapsulated his vision in his opening speech to the team. His message, titled *"Many Boats to One Ship,"* set the tone for unity, resilience, and shared purpose. This is how he described his process of using the framework:

"I was struggling to write my 'big speech' to a bunch of people, many who were pissed off by the closure of their old place of work, some that were new and starry-eyed, and many that would rather have been made redundant. This included many of my management team.

So, I decided to use the UB framework like a jelly-mould,

pouring into it the flavour of jelly that would support the unification process".

We will review and analyse Allan's speech in detail once we've covered all the USIs.

USI 4: **D**efine Actions

With barriers broken down, shared values established, and vision communicated, the next USI in *the* framework is to translate that vision into reality by defining specific actions. Defining actions operates at both broad and detailed levels, transforming vision into reality whether through large-scale initiatives or individual team tasks. This flexibility ensures that each team member has a clear sense of purpose and direction, aligning daily efforts with overarching goals.

For instance, defining actions for the new DC could include creating a roadmap for the training programme, setting milestones for semi-automated system integration, and establishing channels for regular progress feedback. Each action provides clarity, making the transition process more manageable and ensuring that every team member knows their role in the shared journey.

Key Insight: *Defining actions transforms vision into reality. By outlining specific steps, leaders provide clarity, reducing ambiguity and ensuring that every team member understands their role in the collective journey.*

USI 5: **G**et Commitment

Now that actions have been defined, the next USI is to ensure commitment. Commitment-building is a fractal process, where leaders build dedication not only to broad initiatives but also in specific settings like meetings, training sessions, and individual check-ins. This approach transforms commitment from a passive agreement into an active engagement with the team's shared goals.

Building commitment in the new DC can involve a variety of methods, from informal discussions where team members voice their hesitations to formal agreements on shared goals. This creates an environment where everyone is actively participating, strengthening unity through each interaction and ensuring accountability.

Key Insight: *Commitment turns unity into a cohesive force. By fostering genuine buy-in, leaders transform passive agreement into active engagement, ensuring that the team's energy is consistently aligned with its goals.*

USI 6: **E**xcite to Act Now

The final USI in this framework is perhaps the most immediate: Excite to Act Now. Enthusiasm and motivation are core elements that energise teams at every scale, from setting milestones on major projects to fostering enthusiasm in daily tasks. By applying these principles in all interactions, leaders ensure that the team's energy translates into progress, sustaining unity and direction.

For example, setting short-term goals—such as achieving a specific milestone in the semi-automation process—can create immediate momentum and highlight the team's progress. Recognising early successes in team meetings or individual conversations helps maintain enthusiasm, reinforcing unity with each achievement.

Key Insight: *Excitement and urgency turn unity into momentum. By creating a sense of immediate purpose, leaders ensure that the team's energy translates into tangible progress, propelling them forward on their shared path.*

Unity BRIDGE in Action

Here is Allan's speech[2], a direct example of how a unification vision can be communicated with empathy, inclusiveness, and clarity:

Speech Excerpt: "Many Boats to One Ship"

Good morning, everyone.

Today marks the opening of this new distribution centre—a milestone for the company and a big step for all of us here. It's the first day in our new workplace, one that brings with it lots of changes.

For many of us, these changes have stirred up mixed emotions. I want to address those feelings openly because I know this journey hasn't been easy, and I believe that by acknowledging the challenges together, we can steer our way through them.

First, let's acknowledge the obvious—some of us are here from different centres that were closed to make this one possible. We have colleagues who are no longer with us due to redundancies, some who didn't want to leave and others who did.

This situation has created uncertainty, and I understand that many of you may still be adjusting. You're not alone in feeling that way. Each of us has had to adapt, and it's normal to feel some strain and disorientation.

But I ask that we look at this as an opportunity. Today, we're coming out of many boats to one ship. This ship—the new DC—isn't just going to be a place of work; it's going to be a community where every person here, regardless of their role, brings something valuable.

Our shared values—resilience, respect, and quality—are what unite us, regardless of title or tenure.

My vision is simple and ambitious: to become not just a well-oiled machine but a supportive, innovative, and resilient team that becomes the standard for efficiency and collaboration in our business.

Think about a future where we're not just adapting to new systems but we're first in class in operating them, where each of us feels free to contribute ideas, offer solutions, and grow alongside this centre.

To start, we have a few initial steps to ease the transition: comprehensive training sessions, regular check-ins, and open channels for feedback. I urge each of you to engage fully, take part in these activities, and bring your strengths to the table. You have my commitment, and the commitment of every manager and supervisor here, to support you and to ensure that your voice is heard.

Together, we're building a workplace that we can all be proud of, one where our combined efforts will not only create a better environment for us but set an example in our industry. Let's make today the start of a new journey, a shared journey, where we move forward, not as a loose collection of boats, but as one united ship.

Thank you.

To UNDERLINE, Allan wasn't a professional speechwriter: he was an operations leader. His words and sentiment were simple, clear and to the point. Yet, by using the framework, he gave himself the psychological permission to:

- Surrender to the framework's overall USI structure, including their sequence
    - Focus on the things he wanted to say personally, within each of the USIs, to this particular assortment of managers, supervisors and shopfloor workers, in that particular business unit, at that particular moment in time.

Allan's talk not only exemplifies the mission of *engaging for unity*, it highlights the framework's fractal characteristics: not only can the USIs be used to structure the communications strategy and develop a dashboard of KPIs. It was also used to compose the speech. As this pattern was allowed to be replicated at these different scales, a cohesive and adaptable narrative structure emerged.

Later in the transition, there were a few key milestone moments. Some milestones had gone well, some not so well. At these moments, Allan and his leadership team leaned on the framework for these high-impact moments.

As Allan put it:

"Retaining cohesion amongst stakeholders when the news is good is a lot easier than when the results are poor. We used the UB structure regardless. The focus was always on working together better, being true to the principles and priorities, and moving in the right direction as a unit.

> *If the results were great, we talked about unity, commitment and pride in our work. If the results were poor, we did the same. We presented our outcomes this way to the business, to ourselves and to the shopfloor."*

How Allan's Speech Influences the Hive Mind

Allan's speech effectively engages all three levels of the Triune Brain (reptilian survival instincts, mammalian bonding emotions and primate cognition), which influence how groups respond behaviourally. By crafting his message in a way that resonates with these levels, Allan not only communicated his vision but also inspired action and built trust across the organisation.

1. Break Down Barriers

- *Instinct*: Allan acknowledges the uncertainty and strain caused by redundancies and site closures, addressing the team's basic survival fears. This transparency helps reduce the instinctual defensiveness and fight-or-flight responses that often accompany significant change.
- *Emotion*: By validating mixed emotions and shared struggles, Allan builds an empathetic connection, fostering emotional safety and reducing feelings of isolation or resentment.
- *Cognition*: Allan uses clear, logical language to explain the reasons behind the changes, offering a coherent narrative that helps the team intellectually process the situation and see a path forward.

2. Rally Around Shared Values

- *Instinct*: Shared values like resilience, respect, and quality act as grounding principles, providing a sense of stability in a time of upheaval. These values align with the brain's need for safety and predictability.
- *Emotion*: Allan reinforces emotional bonds by highlighting how these values unite the team, creating a shared identity that fosters belonging and trust.
- *Cognition*: The articulation of shared values also engages higher-order thinking, helping team members connect their roles and tasks to broader organisational goals and cultural ideals.

3. Inspire with Vision

- *Instinct*: The metaphor of "many boats to one ship" speaks to the primal need for security and unity, reassuring the team that they are stronger together in navigating the uncertain "seas" ahead.
- *Emotion*: The imagery of working together on a shared journey evokes a sense of camaraderie and collective purpose, appealing to the emotional drive for connection and support.
- *Cognition*: Allan's ambitious vision—becoming a "well-oiled machine" and an industry leader—challenges the team intellectually, inspiring them to think beyond immediate challenges and strive for excellence.

4. Define Actions

- *Instinct*: Outlining tangible steps like training sessions and feedback channels provides the team with a sense of control

and direction, reducing uncertainty and instinctual resistance to change.
- *Emotion*: These actionable steps demonstrate Allan's commitment to supporting the team, fostering trust and reinforcing the emotional bond between leader and team.
- *Cognition*: The clear roadmap satisfies the need for logic and structure, helping the team intellectually understand how their efforts contribute to achieving the vision.

5. Get Commitment

- *Instinct*: By inviting engagement and participation, Allan reduces the instinctual fear of being left behind or overlooked, encouraging active involvement rather than passive compliance.
- *Emotion*: The call for commitment is framed as a mutual pledge, strengthening emotional ties and creating a sense of shared responsibility and accountability.
- *Cognition*: Allan's emphasis on collaboration and contribution appeals to the team's rational side, encouraging them to think critically about how they can add value to the organisation's goals.

6. Excite to Act Now

- *Instinct*: Allan's rallying tone generates energy and urgency, tapping into the team's instinctual drive to take immediate action and "move forward."
- *Emotion*: Celebrating the start of a shared journey reinforces emotional investment, making the team feel valued and motivated to contribute.
- *Cognition*: The focus on building a workplace to be proud of challenges the team to think long-term, aligning their

immediate actions with a broader vision of success and innovation.

Why the Speech Resonates Across the Triune Brain

1. *Balanced Engagement*: Allan ensures his message appeals to instincts, emotions, and intellect, creating a multi-dimensional narrative that resonates deeply with his diverse audience.
2. *Emotional Safety*: By addressing fears and validating emotions, he disarms the instinctual resistance to change while fostering trust and connection.
3. *Visionary Clarity*: Allan provides both the "why" (shared values and vision) and the "how" (tangible actions and commitment), satisfying the team's intellectual need for clarity and coherence.
4. *Motivational Energy*: His concluding call to action inspires immediate engagement, aligning the team's instincts, emotions, and logic toward a shared purpose.

Because Unity BRIDGE is derived from PACE Storytelling's structure, Allan's speech embodies it. His speech begins with a clear acknowledgment of the emotional challenges of redundancies and closures, which fosters safety, builds trust and evokes psychological permission. He encouraged agency over the group survival instincts by reframing the transition as an opportunity for growth, empowering the team to move beyond instinctual defensiveness toward purposeful engagement.

By rallying the team around shared values like resilience, respect, and quality, and using the unifying metaphor of "many boats to one ship," he created emotional connection and strengthened group cohesion. Finally, Allan embeds a new narrative of collaboration and progress through a clear vision and actionable steps, replacing uncertainty with unity, momentum and shared purpose.

KEY TAKEAWAY

Allan's speech is a masterclass in narrative leadership, effectively targeting the Triune Brain to foster unity, resilience, and forward momentum. By engaging instincts, emotions, and intellect, he creates a multi-layered message that aligns his team's collective efforts with a shared vision, ensuring the new distribution centre starts its journey on a solid foundation.

As we conclude *Band of Brothers*, it's worth reflecting on the bigger picture. Each USI in this framework builds safety, aligns team members, and creates a unified force that is resilient to disruption. This is not a method for resolving disputes—though its fractal nature means that the core themes within the narrative frame as well as the USIs can be employed effectively in the conflict resolution process. Rather it is a means of creating an environment where individuals feel safe, valued, and motivated to contribute to a shared mission. In doing so, it makes the group's collective 'vagal brake' stronger—more antifragile, less likely to fail.

Not every leadership moment starts with unity. Some begin in discord, inertia, or even despair. How do you lead when the road ahead is unclear? When the past holds more gravity than the future? How do you turn frustration into momentum, resistance into renewal?

This is not just about managing a team—it's about leading through turbulence, when certainty is a luxury and doubt is the default. The next chapter, "Les Misérables", will explore the art of leading through adversity—when where we are is not where we want to be. Because knowing what we do not want is not the same as knowing where we must go. And in those moments, the right story isn't just a tool—it's the turning point.

NINE
"LES MISÉRABLES"

> *The field of narrative in organizations is a new discipline that draws on many traditional sources but is neither confined nor represented by those traditions*[1]
> **Dave Snowden**

"LES MISÉRABLES" is a novel written by Victor Hugo in 1862, which later inspired numerous adaptations, including films, stage productions, and one of the world's most famous musicals. Its enduring legacy across different media reflects its universal themes of redemption, tenacity and justice. It was chosen as the title for this chapter because it symbolises the transformative power of leadership and narratives to turn despair and adversity into unity, resilience, and progress.

Many leaders earn their reputation by transforming dire circumstances into opportunities for renewal and growth. Through talent, vision, and resolve, they guide their people from despair to stability, laying the foundation for new beginnings. Their legacies endure because they inspire generations with narratives of resilience and hope.

Some dismiss storytelling as mere rhetoric, believing that leadership rests on strategy and execution. But history shows that movements are not sustained by policies alone. People do not rally around spreadsheets—they rally around stories that give meaning to their struggle. A leader who fails to provide a compelling narrative does not merely lack inspiration; they forfeit control over the collective imagination of their people.

Figures like Nelson Mandela, Mahatma Gandhi and Abraham Lincoln illustrate the power of leadership to unite fractured societies. Mandela, speaking during his 1964 trial, transformed personal struggle into a collective vision for justice:

"I have walked that long road to freedom. I have tried not to falter; I have made missteps along the way. But I have discovered the secret that after climbing a great hill, one only finds that there are many more hills to climb. With freedom comes responsibilities, and I dare not linger, for my long walk is not ended."[2]

Gandhi, during India's independence struggle, stirred a divided nation with urgency and resolve:

"Here is a mantra I give you: 'Do or Die.' We shall either free India or die in the attempt; we shall not live to see the perpetuation of our slavery.[3]*"*

At Gettysburg, Lincoln transformed a devastating Civil War into a call for unity and democracy, beginning:

> *"Four score and seven years ago, our fathers brought forth on this continent a new nation, conceived in Liberty, and dedicated to the proposition that all men are created equal.*[4]*"*

These leaders wielded words to inspire resilience and collective action, reminding us that even in the darkest moments, a compelling narrative, backed by vision, can ignite transformation.

Today's leaders face an increasingly complex, fast-changing world, they need flexible frameworks to provide structure for creating unity and guiding teams through uncertainty. In dark and difficult moments, narratives are not merely speeches; they align and energise people, addressing gut, heart, and head needs. Without a unifying alternative, human nature gravitates toward division—tribalism, territorialism, and groupthink—creating silos, ideological fractures, or sectarian tensions.

By employing storytelling frameworks, leaders can rebuild trust, align values, and transform fragmented teams into resilient groups capable of thriving through adversity. Impactful leadership is not just about solving problems but about telling stories that inspire collective progress and resilience.

The 4Cs of Effective Leadership

Throughout history there have been moments of immense challenge. From fractured societies to oppressive regimes and national crises, these moments called for leaders with the qualities necessary to inspire unity, resilience, and progress. They required leadership that was not just about what had to be done but how it all was communicated.

Inspiring leaders share four fundamental qualities. First, they demonstrate _compassion_, recognising and addressing the emotions of those they lead to build trust and connection. Second, they establish _credibility_, earning trust through authenticity and integrity so that their words carry weight. Third, they apply _cognition_, framing challenges with clarity and insight to help others navigate complexity. Finally, they lead through _campaign_, rallying collective energy toward a shared mission, transforming vision into action. These qualities shape narratives that do not merely describe the world as it is but envision it as it could be.

Take Nelson Mandela. His speech during his trial in 1964 was a masterclass in *compassion*, as he validated the pain of oppression while offering hope for the future. His unwavering *credibility* stemmed from his personal sacrifices, which aligned his words with his deeds. By articulating the fight for justice with clarity (*cognition*), he transformed despair into resolve. And through his call to action, he united a nation under a campaign for freedom.

Similarly, Mahatma Gandhi's leadership during India's independence movement was rooted in *compassion* for the suffering of millions, paired with an unshakeable commitment to nonviolence (*credibility*). His speeches clarified the stakes of their struggle (*cognition*) and rallied the people to a campaign of sacrifice and determination: "Do or Die."

Abraham Lincoln's *Gettysburg Address* encapsulated these same qualities. With humility and grace, he connected with a grieving nation (*compassion*), rooted his words in democratic ideals (*credibility*), and framed the Civil War as a fight for equality and unity (*cognition*). His resolve to see the nation reborn as a government "of the people, by the people, for the people" became the campaign that carried the United States forward.

From Timeless Principles *to Practical Framework*

While Mandela, Gandhi, and Lincoln shaped the course of nations, today's leaders must navigate equally complex human dynamics in workplaces, communities, and organisations. The challenge is no longer just about shaping national movements but about aligning diverse teams, resolving internal tensions, and guiding people through uncertainty. The question is not whether we will face crises, but how we will lead our teams through them. This is where structured narrative tools like *FOCUS UP* become essential.

This framework incorporates the elements of the 4Cs into the PACE Storytelling framework for high engagement and impact[5]. It is a practical tool that helps leaders guide their people through uncertainty, fostering unity and resilience while inspiring the collective action needed to move from adversity to opportunity. By structuring communication around these principles, leaders can turn paralysis into momentum, ensuring that their teams not only survive challenges but emerge stronger.

Whether addressing a missed target, navigating a hostile stakeholder meeting, or leading a team through market upheaval, *FOCUS UP* equips leaders to reframe adversity, inspire belief, and rally efforts toward a shared vision. It transforms the timeless lessons of historic leadership into actionable steps, enabling today's leaders to inspire their teams to journey toward—and build—something better.

FRAMEWORK Overview

The adaptive framework offers leaders a clear roadmap for navigating uncertainty with clarity, empathy, and purpose. It is designed to address the instinctual, emotional, and rational needs of teams, transforming confusion into confidence and inertia into action. The framework comprises seven interconnected components, each targeting a specific facet of leadership communication:

1. **F***rame the Context*: Establish a shared understanding of the situation, eliminating ambiguity and aligning perspectives.
2. **O***bserve Shared Experiences*: Validate emotions and foster empathy, ensuring team members feel seen, heard, and connected.
3. **C***oncretise the Challenge*: Define the specific problem, channelling energy toward manageable and actionable goals.
4. **U***plift with Vision*: Present a hopeful and realistic future, inspiring the team to view the challenge as a pathway to growth.
5. **S***et the Steps*: Outline clear, tangible actions that bridge the gap between the current state and the desired outcome.
6. **U***nite Their Hearts*: Anchor actions in shared values, forging a deeper emotional commitment to the mission.
7. **P***ress for Action*: Turn alignment and energy into purposeful momentum, ensuring decisive forward movement.

These components form a flexible narrative arc, addressing both immediate challenges and long-term aspirations. Unlike rigid, linear models such as Kotter's Eight-Step Process, *this process* is fluid and iterative. Leaders can activate its elements simultaneously or shift focus as conditions evolve, maintaining balance and momentum across the team.

To fully appreciate the potential of this framework, it's important to understand its fractal nature—a characteristic that enables it to adapt dynamically to challenges at any scale.

Group Safety Rupture Repair

At its heart, FOCUS UP isn't just a structural tool—it's a way to repair safety ruptures at the group level. Leaders who effectively employ the framework guide their teams on a journey from negative emotions like fear, helplessness, and despair, toward positive states like trust, empowerment and hope.

This emotional transformation is not accidental; it is deeply rooted in the PACE Storytelling framework from which it was derived. PACE's phases guide the shifts in their states, ensuring the group moves intentionally through vulnerability, empowerment, connection and renewal. By adapting these principles, the framework transforms fragmented or fearful teams into cohesive and motivated units. Each step actively addresses the instincts, emotions, and cognition of the group, ensuring the transformation from safety rupture to resilience is not only possible but predictable.

Using PACE as a foundation, the emotional arc within FOCUS UP can be made explicit:

1. ***Permission***: At the outset, leaders establish psychological safety by validating fears and anxieties. By acknowledging the shared challenges that people face (e.g., through Frame the Context and Observe Shared Experiences), leaders defuse defensiveness and create openness to dialogue.
    - Emotional Transition: From defensiveness to openness.
2. ***Agency***: By framing challenges as surmountable and providing actionable steps forward (Concretise the Challenge and Set the Steps), leaders empower teams to

shift from passive helplessness to active engagement. Reframing adversity as an opportunity for growth taps into the team's instinctual drive for survival, channelling it into purposeful action.
    - Emotional Transition: From helplessness to empowerment.
3. **Connection**: Teams often begin in fragmented or isolated states, exacerbating uncertainty. By fostering emotional resonance through shared values and experiences (Observe Shared Experiences and Unite Their Hearts), leaders cultivate a sense of connection and belonging, reducing anxiety and creating trust.
    - Emotional Transition: From isolation to connection.
4. **Embedding**: Finally, leaders solidify the emotional transformation by offering a vision of hope and progress (Uplift with Vision) and translating it into tangible action (Press for Action). By doing so, they redefine current struggles as stepping stones toward a brighter, collective future, replacing despair with optimism and determination.
    - Emotional Transition: From despair to hope.

The framework is not just about organising ideas or clarifying actions; it's about repairing disconnected states, fostering connection, cohesion, and unity. The framework leverages the PACE Storytelling structure to address and guide instinctual, emotional, and cognitive responses, ensuring teams feel safe, connected and inspired.

Each USI is designed to move teams along this emotional arc; by monitoring these USIs diligently and taking corrective action, leaders maintain the group's unity. In doing so, leaders can transform negative instinctual states into positive emotional states, enabling the full cognitive capacity of the group to problem-solve and flourish together.

Narratives do not merely define the present; they shape the future. A great leader's story is never static—it evolves, responding to challenges, crises and transformations. The leader who understands this does not merely react to circumstances but actively reshapes them through the power of narrative. This is not a one-time process but an *ongoing practice* of storytelling, adaptation, and influence.

The Fractal Nature

The framework is not a rigid, linear process; instead, it mirrors the complexity and adaptability of living systems. Its fractal nature lies in its ability to be applied consistently across varying scales—whether in addressing a crisis affecting an entire organisation, resolving tensions within a team, or guiding a one-on-one conversation with a colleague. At every level, the same principles and Unity-Stabilising Inputs (USIs) remain relevant, yet they adapt dynamically to the context.

- **Core Consistency Across Scales**
  - Just as fractals exhibit self-similar patterns regardless of scale, the framework provides a stable structure that works across micro and macro levels. For example:
  - At the *organisational level*, "Frame the Context" might involve addressing the entire workforce about a restructuring initiative.
  - At the *team level*, it could mean clarifying specific project roles and goals to ensure alignment.
  - At the *individual level*, it might involve acknowledging a colleague's unique struggles and aligning on shared objectives. Despite the difference in scope, the same process of aligning understanding and setting a foundation for action applies.
- **Adaptability to Complexity**

- Leadership challenges often resemble complex adaptive systems: they are dynamic, interconnected, and unpredictable. The fractal nature of this framework enables leaders to navigate this complexity by breaking large challenges into smaller, manageable pieces. Each USI can be applied iteratively and repeatedly, scaling up or down as necessary, while maintaining alignment with the broader vision.

Fractals in Action

- **Crisis Management at Different Scales**
    - *Macro-Level*: A CEO addressing the company during a major market disruption used FOCUS UP to Frame the Context of economic uncertainty, Concretise the Challenge of declining sales, and Uplift with Vision for pivoting to new markets.
    - *Micro-Level*: A team leader within that same organisation used the framework to Frame the Context of adapting to new KPIs, Observe Shared Experiences of team fatigue, and Press for Action to prioritise short-term goals.
- **Iterative Implementation**
    - Each USI can be revisited multiple times within a single initiative:
    - *Framing the Context* might evolve as new information emerges, requiring leaders to re-establish shared understanding at each stage.
    - *Uniting Their Hearts* might need reinforcement to sustain morale over time, particularly during prolonged or complex projects.

Fractals & Feedback Loops

In complex systems, feedback loops help maintain balance. Similarly, the fractal nature of FOCUS UP incorporates continuous feedback:

- Leaders can revisit earlier USIs as new challenges or opportunities arise.
- For instance, after implementing steps to address an immediate problem, a leader may need to return to "Observe Shared Experiences" to reassess team morale and make adjustments.

Why Fractals Matter in Leadership

1. *Scalability*: The framework provides leaders with a single tool that can be scaled up or down without losing its core utility.
2. *Sustainability*: Its iterative application ensures adaptability over time, supporting sustained progress rather than one-time fixes.
3. *Resonance*: By maintaining consistency across different levels, the framework builds trust and alignment, as team members see coherent leadership in every interaction.

Much like a fractal design in nature—a fern leaf or a coastline—the framework reflects the patterns of human communication and collaboration. It adapts dynamically to challenges and scales seamlessly, ensuring leaders can address the big picture while never losing sight of the details.

Key Insight: The fractal nature of the framework reinforces its effectiveness in addressing both the complexity and nuance of leadership. Leaders who internalise this concept can seamlessly apply the framework across diverse contexts, ensuring clarity, alignment, and progress at every level of their organisation or team.

Having explored the adaptability of the framework, let us now examine how these principles manifest in real-world scenarios, showcasing the power of narrative to align, inspire, and propel action.

ADAPTABILITY FOR DIVERSE Scenarios

The strength of narrative framework lies in its adaptability. It's not limited to large-scale transformations or formal presentations. It can be seamlessly applied to diverse contexts, such as:

- *Engagement Framework* for internal and external stakeholder engagement
- *One-on-One Conversations*: Supporting a team member through personal or professional challenges.
- *Team Huddles*: Realigning priorities and boosting morale during periods of high stress.
- *Ad Hoc Problem-Solving*: Quickly framing context and solutions in moments of crisis.

Whether addressing a workforce after a major setback, engaging stakeholders during organisational change, or navigating periods of high-pressure situations, the framework scales to meet the unique demands of each moment.

At its core, *the framework* builds trust and momentum. By balancing transparency with inspiration, it equips leaders to address challenges constructively while maintaining sight of the bigger picture. It turns adversity into opportunity, enabling teams to emerge not merely intact but stronger, more united, and better prepared for future challenges.

This is not just a tool for managing crises—it's a method for cultivating resilience and forging progress. By guiding teams through ambiguity and adversity, the framework empowers leaders to create lasting change, uniting people around a shared vision and ensuring forward motion.

***FOCUS UP* Framework**

As with Unity BRIDGE, this framework is fractal in its nature. In this case, the framework provides seven *Unity Stabilising Inputs* (USIs), each addressing a key element of leadership communication. Together, these components guide teams from uncertainty to purposeful action, building trust, clarity, and momentum.

USI 1: **F**rame the Context

Framing the context is the first step in aligning your team. It's more than stating facts—it's about establishing a shared foundation for understanding the situation. Without this, assumptions diverge, leading to confusion and conflict.

Framing the context is like orienting a map. Before determining the destination, you must clarify where you are. Without this reference point, a team risks heading in the wrong direction.

Tone is as critical as content. Leaders who catastrophise can spark panic, while those who sugar-coat risk complacency. Effective framing strikes a balance: presenting the truth with composure, clarity, and confidence.

For instance, an operations leader addressing a severe backlog began:

> *"We've faced challenges—resource shortages, client demands, and system failures—but your resilience has kept us going. Now, for the first time, the backlog is shrinking. We're gaining momentum, and I know we can clear this together"*

This leader acknowledged the difficulty without exaggeration, celebrated progress, and set a positive tone. Transparency like this reinforces psychological safety and aligns the team.

> **Key Insight**: Framing the context grounds the team in reality, fostering clarity and reducing ambiguity. With a shared understanding, teams are better equipped to focus on solutions.

USI 2: **O**bserve Shared Experiences

Acknowledging emotions is crucial for unity. Leaders who validate team members' feelings foster psychological safety and empathy, helping to build trust and camaraderie.

Emotions in a team are like unseen ocean currents—if ignored, they can pull the team off course. By recognising and sharing these experiences, leaders steer with empathy, creating a supportive environment.

For example, during the height of COVID-19, a factory owner told their team:

> *"I know many of you are exhausted. The shortages and delays have tested us all. But know this: your dedication is what's keeping us afloat, and we'll get through this together."*

This simple acknowledgment validated the team's effort and emotions, reinforcing trust and a sense of shared purpose.

Key Insight: Observing shared experiences builds an emotional bridge. Recognising and validating team struggles fosters resilience and strengthens group cohesion.

USI 3: Concretise the Challenge

Turning vague concerns into actionable problems helps focus the team's energy. Concretising the challenge shifts the narrative from emotional overwhelm to productive clarity.

A factory manager facing a 168% surge in demand addressed her team:

> *"Our orders have quadrupled, and we need to adapt quickly. First, we'll reset client expectations. Then, we'll ramp up overtime and improve workflows. Let's focus on stabilising operations while exploring long-term capacity solutions"*

This clarity redirected the team from feeling overwhelmed to addressing tangible tasks, transforming anxiety into agency.

Key Insight: Concretising the challenge channels energy into action. A clear, objective focus minimises blame and defensiveness, fostering an environment for problem-solving.

USI 4: **U**plift with Vision

A compelling vision shifts focus from immediate challenges to future possibilities, inspiring hope and energising the team.

A leader's vision acts like a lighthouse in a storm—it doesn't calm the waves but provides a guiding light. Effective visions are inclusive, balancing clarity with room for team contributions.

After defining a capacity challenge, a factory manager said:

> *"Imagine a workplace with optimised workflows, state-of-the-art tools, and flexible schedules. That's our future, and your creativity and resilience will get us there"*

This vision connected short-term struggles to a greater purpose, motivating the team with a shared goal.

> ***Key Insight***: Vision connects present struggles to a brighter future. By offering realistic hope and inclusivity, leaders inspire collective action.

USI 5: **S**et the Steps

To turn vision into reality, leaders must outline clear, actionable steps. Without this, even the most inspiring vision risks feeling unattainable.

Beth, the factory manager, told her team:

> *"Here's our plan: First, we'll connect with the key customers. Next,*

we'll identify workflow bottlenecks for quick wins. Finally, we'll scope long-term capacity expansions, with input from all of you"

Breaking tasks into manageable steps creates clarity and accountability, giving the team confidence in their ability to progress[6].

> ***Key Insight***: Setting the steps translates vision into action. By defining clear tasks and ensuring accountability, leaders provide a roadmap that bridges present struggles and future success.

USI 6: **U**nite Their Hearts

While logic informs decisions, it is emotion that drives commitment. Leaders who unite their team's hearts create a shared identity, transforming individual efforts into collective purpose.

A healthcare leader told their team:

> *"No matter the changes, our commitment to dignity and compassion remains. Together, we're not just meeting challenges; we're shaping a future aligned with our values"*

Anchoring actions in shared values strengthens emotional bonds and commitment, fostering unity and resilience.

> ***Key Insight***: Uniting hearts appeals to shared values, inspiring genuine emotional commitment. Authenticity and

consistency from leaders build trust and reinforce group identity.

USI 7: **P**ress for Action

The final step turns alignment into momentum. Pressing for action provides the spark to translate preparation into progress.

A manufacturing leader concluded their address:

> *"We've done the groundwork. By week's end, I want each team to submit recommendations for streamlining workflows. Let's take the first step today"*

Urgency and achievable goals create momentum, while celebrating early wins sustains motivation.

> ***Key Insight***: Pressing for action converts unity into progress. Leaders who set clear starting points and create urgency ensure immediate, purposeful motion.

Practical Applications

The framework is dynamic and scalable, applicable in various scenarios:

- *One-on-One*: Reconnecting disengaged team members by observing shared struggles and setting clear goals.

- *Team Huddles:* Aligning a team during stress with clear context and concrete steps.
- *Large-Scale Presentations:* Inspiring alignment across diverse groups with vision and decisive action.

FOCUS UP equips leaders to transform uncertainty into clarity and challenges into opportunities, ensuring progress even in the most adverse conditions.

Douglas's Team Address

"Good morning, everyone.

Earlier this week, something happened that we can't ignore. Many of you witnessed Jerry's incident. He froze—physically, mentally, emotionally. He couldn't move, speak, or act.

Stress got to him. It built up silently over time until his body shut down. Jerry isn't injured, but what he went through should remind us all of how much pressure we carry in this job—and how dangerous it can be if we don't address it.

This isn't just Jerry's story; it's a story about all of us[7]. Who here hasn't felt that weight? The pressure to hit targets, keep everything running smoothly, and not let anyone down? It impacts all of us differently, but when one of us breaks, it's a sign that something deeper needs to change.

Let me ask you to imagine a different kind of workplace. One where we don't wait until someone reaches their breaking point. One where it's safe to speak up, to say, 'I'm not okay,' before it's too late. A place where leaders, myself included, notice when someone is struggling and step in with real support. Can you picture that?

We can build that place, but it's going to take all of us. Starting today, we'll be making some changes. First, we're introducing regular check-

ins so we can talk honestly about what's working and not working. Next, we'll be rolling out training for leaders to spot the early signs of stress and act before things escalate. And most importantly, we'll put well-being on par with productivity. That means creating a culture where trust and safety come first.

This isn't just about reducing stress. It's about becoming the kind of team that lifts each other up, a team that thrives under pressure without breaking. Let's commit, together, to making this change. Let's make safety—not just physical but mental—a priority. When we do, we'll not only become stronger as individuals but unstoppable as a team".

The Effect on His *Hive's Mind*

Douglas's speech artfully engages all three levels of the Triune Brain (reptilian survival instincts, mammalian bonding emotions, and primate cognition), creating a narrative that fosters trust, unity, and purposeful action. By addressing these layers, Douglas transforms a moment of vulnerability into a catalyst for resilience and collective progress[8].

1. **Frame the Context**
    - *Instinct*: Douglas begins by addressing the immediate survival concern—stress-induced breakdowns like Jerry's incident. This acknowledgment calms the primal fear of instability and danger by signalling that the leader recognises the issue and is taking control.
    - *Emotion*: By connecting Jerry's experience to a shared team reality, Douglas validates the collective emotional struggle, reducing feelings of isolation and fostering psychological safety.
    - *Cognition*: Framing the context as a reflection of deeper systemic issues shifts the focus from individual blame to

a broader intellectual understanding of the problem, creating clarity and shared perspective.

2. **Observe Shared Experiences**
    - *Instinct*: Douglas explicitly acknowledges the pressure everyone feels, reducing instinctual defensiveness by showing that struggles are recognised and normalised.
    - *Emotion*: Validating the team's emotional burden builds empathy and connection, making team members feel seen, heard, and supported.
    - *Cognition*: By linking individual stress to a collective reality, Douglas helps the team intellectually understand how shared challenges affect them as a group, fostering alignment.

3. **Concretise the Challenge**
    - *Instinct*: Defining the challenge as a culture that prioritises productivity over well-being reassures the team that the problem is tangible and solvable, addressing primal fears of unpredictability.
    - *Emotion*: Douglas shifts the narrative from overwhelming stress to actionable change, giving the team emotional relief and a sense of agency.
    - *Cognition*: Clearly articulating the systemic issue allows the team to focus on logical, constructive solutions rather than being paralysed by uncertainty.

4. **Uplift with Vision**
    - *Instinct*: Douglas paints a vision of a workplace where safety and well-being are prioritised, appealing to the primal desire for security and stability.
    - *Emotion*: His aspirational vision of trust and support inspires hope and emotional investment, motivating the team to believe in a better future.
    - *Cognition*: The vision connects the team's current struggles to a long-term goal, encouraging them to think

critically about how their efforts contribute to this transformation

5. **Set the Steps**
   - *Instinct*: Concrete actions like check-ins, leader training, and a well-being culture provide a roadmap, reducing uncertainty and satisfying the need for control and direction.
   - *Emotion*: The actionable steps demonstrate leadership commitment, strengthening trust and emotional buy-in.
   - *Cognition*: Outlining clear steps transforms the vision into a logical, achievable plan, empowering the team with clarity and purpose.

6. **Unite Their Hearts**
   - *Instinct*: Anchoring the new culture in shared values like teamwork and mutual support are strong cues of safety, obviating primal responses.
   - *Emotion*: Douglas appeals to the team's emotional connection to their shared mission, reinforcing bonds and a sense of collective identity.
   - *Cognition*: Highlighting shared values aligns individual goals with the team's broader purpose, fostering intellectual and moral commitment.

7. **Press for Action**
   - *Instinct*: Douglas's direct call to action activates the team's survival-driven need for immediate progress, providing momentum and focus.
   - *Emotion*: His emphasis on collective commitment energises the team, creating a sense of urgency and shared responsibility.
   - *Cognition*: By clearly linking the call to action with specific steps, Douglas ensures logical alignment between the team's efforts and the desired outcome.

Triune Brain Resonation

1. *Instinctual Engagement*: Douglas addresses fears of stress and burnout by acknowledging vulnerabilities, outlining practical steps, and providing a vision of safety, thereby reducing fight-or-flight responses.
2. *Emotional Connection*: Through empathy and validation, he strengthens bonds within the team, creating a supportive environment that fosters trust and collaboration.
3. *Intellectual Clarity*: By framing the problem clearly, providing a roadmap, and connecting actions to values, Douglas satisfies the team's need for logical understanding and purpose.

Key Takeaway: Douglas's speech demonstrates the power of narrative to address the Triune Brain holistically, transforming a crisis into an opportunity for growth. By engaging instincts, emotions, and intellect, he builds trust, inspires action, and aligns the team around a shared vision of resilience and progress. His structured use of the framework ensures the message resonates at every level, fostering a culture of safety, unity, and forward momentum.

OTHER NARRATIVE APPLICATIONS

The flexibility of the framework extends beyond formal speeches, enabling leaders to address diverse scenarios, from brief conversations to team meetings and organisational presentations:

- *Brief Interactions*: For a disengaged team member, a leader might *Frame the Context* by acknowledging recent pressures, *Observe Shared Experiences* by validating their struggles, and *Set the Steps* for improvement with clear, supportive actions.
- *Meetings*: In tense discussions, leaders can *Frame the Context* to align the group, *Concretise the Challenge* to clarify focus, and *Unite Their Hearts* around shared goals, ensuring the meeting remains productive and aligned.
- *Presentations*: When launching new initiatives, leaders can *Uplift with Vision* to inspire belief and *Press for Action* to energise the audience into taking decisive steps forward.

The adaptability of FOCUS UP makes it indispensable for leaders working within complex, living systems. Whether addressing a crisis, facilitating discussions, or rallying a team, the framework's *Unity-Stabilising Inputs* (USIs) counteract the tendency toward disunity and destabilising feedback loops. It reinforces focus, resilience, and alignment, ensuring leadership communication drives meaningful and lasting change.

KEY INSIGHTS

> *"The universe is a continuous web. Touch it at any point and the whole web quivers.[9]"*
> **Stanley Kunitz**

In times of strife, leaders are measured not just by their plans or performance but by the narratives they craft—stories that guide, unite, and inspire people to make things better. As we've explored throughout this chapter, narratives are indispensable tools for sense-making, especially in the face of uncertainty, ambiguity, and complexity.

Historic leaders like Nelson Mandela, Mahatma Gandhi, and Abraham Lincoln mastered the art of narrative to connect with their people's instincts, emotions, and cognition. Their speeches were not mere calls to action but transformative moments that reshaped meaning, instilled clarity, and created shared purpose.

In today's volatile and fast-changing world, leaders must similarly harness their own and their teams' instinctual drives. By mastering crafted narrative frameworks, leaders can portray shared experiences, demonstrate compassion, and inspire collective action. The framework provides a way to move people from instability, discomfort or fear toward hope, stability, and renewed purpose. Without such guidance, many would remain stuck in familiar, unproductive patterns.

This framework is more than a crisis management tool—it is a dynamic framework for leading people out of adversity. By aligning with the fluid and adaptive nature of leadership, it offers flexibility across a range of scenarios, from high-stakes speeches to team discussions and one-on-one conversations.

Its true value lies not in rigid linear steps but in its dynamic, *USI-driven approach*, underpinned by the *'4Cs of Effective Leadership'* (compassion, credibility, cognition, and campaign). These aspects ensure leaders remain responsive to the very human complexities that influence team dynamics, enabling them to sustain unity and momentum even in turbulent environments.

As leaders navigate the ever-changing landscapes of their organisations, they must remember that their words shape their legacies. A well-crafted narrative is not merely a strategy; it is a beacon—a light that transforms confusion into clarity, disconnection into unity, and inertia into progress.

Leaders who know how to influence the Hive Mind do not merely solve problems. They tell stories that help others believe in solutions, commit to action, and persevere through uncertainty. The question is not whether you will lead with stories—you already are. The question is whether you will do so *consciously, with precision* and *purpose*. The narratives you craft today will define the reality you and your team will face tomorrow. So—what story will you tell? And who might be changed because you told it?

PART THREE SUMMARY

*Nature always finds a way;
we must simply allow it*
Leonardo da Vinci

Leadership in times of profound change demands far more than technical expertise or meticulous planning. It requires the ability to navigate the uncertain terrain of human instincts, emotions and intellect—a realm where ambiguity thrives and traditional logic falters. Leaders are not merely decision-makers; they are weavers of meaning, capable of crafting stories that cut through the fog of complexity, build unity from fragmentation, and transform fear into hope.

PACE Storytelling, the focus of this part, is a leadership framework that equips individuals to create these transformative narratives. It builds on the foundation of non-verbal leadership explored earlier, adding language as a tool—not just any words, but carefully chosen ones that resonate with the gut, heart and mind.

To understand the power of storytelling in leadership, we must first recognise its dual function. As Dave Snowden articulates, stories serve as mechanisms for 'sense-making'—the process of discerning patterns amidst chaos—and for 'meaning-making'—reframing those patterns to inspire purposeful action. Together, these capabilities make storytelling indispensable for leaders navigating the tangled networks of human systems.

Consider a leader addressing a fractured team, their cohesion eroded by silos and suspicion. A direct command to collaborate may fail to resonate. But a narrative that reframes their predicament as an opportunity to achieve something greater together has the power to unite. This is not storytelling as a 'soft skill'; it is an essential leadership tool, particularly in environments where uncertainty reigns, and human dynamics take centre stage.

Neurological Anchors

Stories are ancient tools that connect our past experiences with present challenges and future possibilities[1]. Their resonance is rooted in the structure of the human brain, as Paul MacLean's *Triune Brain* model so elegantly demonstrates. At the most primal level, stories engage the Reptilian Brain, addressing our survival instincts. Tales of danger narrowly avoided, for instance, trigger visceral responses that prepare us for action, as if we were reliving the moment ourselves.

The Mammalian Brain, responsible for emotion and connection, is drawn to stories of love, loss, and triumph—narratives that build trust and foster shared identity. Finally, the Primate Brain engages with stories that challenge our assumptions and expand our understanding, offering intellectual stimulation and new insights.

Stephen Porges' *Polyvagal Theory* extends this understanding by showing how stories can shift the autonomic nervous system from defensive states (fight, flight, or freeze) to states of social engagement. A narrative that acknowledges collective anxieties while offering reassurance signals safety to the listener, unlocking the emotional and intellectual resources necessary for collaboration and creativity.

Take the archetypal hero's journey as an example. The protagonist faces life-threatening danger, emotional trials and, finally, transformative insight. This enduring narrative resonates because it engages the whole of our humanity: our instincts, our emotions and our intellect. Leaders must take note—a story that appeals only to the intellect may inform but rarely inspires; a story targeting only emotions may lack clarity. The most impactful narratives weave all these elements together into a cohesive whole.

Reframing Adversity

Leadership is often tested most during transitions—when fear and disconnection amplify. Ralph Stacey's insight into the nonlinear nature of human behaviour reminds us that leaders cannot impose order on complex systems. Instead, they must guide people through them by crafting narratives that resonate with lived experience.

Consider a team divided by conflicting priorities and mistrust. A directive to 'work together' is likely to ring hollow. However, a story that highlights shared victories from the past can reframe the current challenges as opportunities to replicate those successes. This act of reframing, grounded in both collective memory and future potential, creates alignment and fosters trust.

Daniel Kahneman's work on framing provides a further dimension. By reshaping how challenges are presented—turning threats into opportunities, for instance—leaders can alter the way their teams perceive adversity, shifting them from paralysis to purpose.

Physiological Arc

The PACE Storytelling framework is not just a method; it is an emotional journey. Its arc transforms states of defensiveness, helplessness and despair into openness, empowerment and hope. The process begins with 'Permission', where leaders validate emotions and create psychological safety. This is the starting point for shifting from defensiveness to openness.

The next phase, *'Agency'* encourages individuals to transcend their reactive instincts, framing challenges as opportunities for choice and action. This transformation replaces helplessness with engagement. In 'Connection', leaders build emotional bonds through shared values and experiences, fostering unity. Finally, the narrative concludes with 'Embedding' by reframing adversity as a catalyst for growth and replacing despair with optimism.

COMPLEXITY & EVOLUTION

PACE is more than a linear framework; it is a living system, reflecting the principles of complex adaptive systems as articulated by Meg Wheatley, Ralph Stacey, and Dave Snowden. Its negative feedback loops—Unity-Stabilising Inputs (USIs)—allow leaders to address multiple dynamics concurrently, dampening adverse developments while maintaining coherence.

Dave Snowden's *Cynefin* framework highlights the importance of adaptable approaches. PACE embodies this adaptability. Whether aligning an entire organisation during a restructuring, guiding a team's project discussions, or addressing individual challenges, PACE provides a scalable structure for coherence and alignment.

Richard Bandler's influence is woven into the very DNA of PACE, particularly his foundational concept of 'pace and lead.' This idea, reframed for leadership contexts, underscores the importance of aligning with a team's current emotional and cognitive state before guiding them toward new possibilities.

Some of Bandler's toolkit was discussed —reframing, nested loops, and metaphors—which he uses to elevate storytelling into a transformative art. *Reframing* allows leaders to shift perspectives, turning obstacles into opportunities. *Nested loops* engage the triune brain, embedding deep insights by weaving multiple stories that resolve in reverse order. *Metaphors* provide leaders with a bridge between abstract concepts and lived experience, making complex ideas tangible and relatable.

These techniques ensure that PACE is not just a framework for storytelling, but a methodology for transforming instincts, emotions, and behaviours in real-world leadership scenarios.

The derivatives of PACE are both diverse and numerous and I have developed many over the years. The two frameworks selected for a detailed unpacking demonstrate its scalability and versatility. Unity BRIDGE focuses on uniting diverse groups, emphasising shared values and collective purpose—essential during transitions like mergers.

FOCUS UP, on the other hand, addresses crises, guiding teams from despair to resilience through visionary leadership and actionable steps. Both frameworks retain PACE's iterative, fractal nature, ensuring adaptability to any challenge.

Leadership is Storytelling

It is the ability to frame and reframe narratives that align instincts, emotions, and intellect, transforming complexity into clarity and disconnection into unity. The PACE Storytelling framework equips leaders with tools to navigate the shifting sands of organisational life, inspiring trust, alignment, and action.

What stories will you tell to guide your teams? How will you craft narratives that resonate with the whole of their humanity? In the end, the stories we tell shape the futures we create—building environments where flourishing, resilience, and unity become possible. And when we look back on our leadership journeys—surely, that's what we hope to have achieved?

Summary of Tools & Techniques

This part presents a series of frameworks and strategies that leaders can use to create *unity, resilience* and *alignment* through storytelling. The frameworks provide structured approaches to sense-making, meaning-making and mobilising action within complex adaptive systems.

- **PACE Storytelling** - helps leaders navigate complexity through narrative framing.
- **Unity BRIDGE** - helps leaders designed for uniting diverse groups and factions.
- **FOCUS UP** - helps leaders navigate out of adversity and crisis by inspiring action.

Story Structures Summary

PACE Storytelling Framework

Purpose: This framework (along with Unity BRIDGE and FOCUS UP) is straightforward to implement. It empowers leaders to navigate complexity through *narrative*, turning chaos into clarity by engaging hidden patterns.

More than a communication tool, it engages the full spectrum of human cognition—resonating viscerally with the Reptilian Brain, fostering trust through the Mammalian Brain, and aligning decisions with the analytical Primate Brain. This makes storytelling a structured approach to sense-making, meaning-making, and deep engagement.

1. Permission

- *Establish group safety* the test for new narrative receptiveness.
- **Action:** Use shared experiences, acknowledging struggles, fears, and concerns.
- **Example:** "Many of you feel uncertainty about the changes ahead. I hear you."

2. Agency

- Reframe the situation to diminish the need for fear and defensiveness.
- **Action:** Highlight collective control; share other times they overcame adversity.
- **Example:** "We've been here before, and each time we've adapted and got better."

3. Connection

- Align individuals with a *collective identity* through shared values and vision.
- **Action:** Use metaphors and stories to unify perspectives.
- **Example:** "Many boats, one ship—we are all navigating these waters together."

4. Embedding

- Ensure the new meanings are reinforced with repeated storytelling.
- **Action:** Use *fractal patterns* for narrative alignment across different scales.
- **Example:** Regular team debriefs for shared narrative perspectives.

Story Arc of PACE

Purpose: Move teams through states to foster safety, cohesion, unity and action.

1. *Self-protection* → *permission*: Validate emotions and reduce resistance.
2. *Powerless* → *Empowerment*: Reframe challenges as opportunities.
3. *Isolation* → *Connection*: Build shared values, goals and experiences.
4. *Old Beliefs* → *New Meanings*: Provide insights to connect the '*As Is*' to the '*To Be*'.

Unity BRIDGE Framework

Purpose: This framework was specifically designed for uniting diverse groups, such as during mergers, reorganisations, or cultural integration efforts.

1. Break Down Barriers

- Address *psychological silos* and emotional divisions.
- **Action:** Encourage cross-department collaboration and shared problem-solving.
- **Example:** "Let's rotate teams in training to learn from diverse experiences".

2. Rally Around Shared Values

- Define a *common cultural foundation* to unify the group.
- **Action:** Identify 3-5 **core values** and integrate them into daily conversations and decisions.
- **Example:** "Respect, resilience, and quality will guide how we work together."

3. Inspire with Vision

- Articulate a *compelling future* that aligns with the shared values.
- **Action:** Use vivid imagery and storytelling to *paint the future*.
- **Example:** "Imagine a centre where we set the standard in the industry for efficiency and collaboration."

4. Define Actions

- Turn abstract vision into *concrete actions*.

- **Action:** Break down the path forward into clear, actionable steps.
- **Example:** "We will start by implementing weekly open forums for feedback."

5. Get Commitment

- Ensure *active participation* rather than passive agreement.
- **Action:** Foster ownership through clear role expectations and accountability measures.
- **Example:** "Each team will assign one ambassador to track our progress and share concerns."

6. Excite to Act Now

- Create *urgency and momentum* to initiate immediate action.
- **Action:** Set short-term milestones and *celebrate early wins*.
- **Example:** "In the first 30 days, let's complete our first project to set the tone for success.

FOCUS UP Framework

Purpose: This framework is designed for navigating adversity and crisis, transforming fear and paralysis into momentum and action.

1. Frame the Context

- Create a *shared understanding* of the situation.
- **Action:** Clearly and accurately state the current reality in ways that is verifiable.
- **Example:** "We're facing an increased workload and fatigue is showing."

2. Observe Shared Experiences

- Validate *team emotions* to build psychological safety.
- **Action:** Share a common struggle to make people feel heard and understood.
- **Example:** "I know many of you feel frustrated. This pressure affects all of us."

3. Concretise the Challenge

- Define the *problem in clear, actionable terms.*
- **Action:** Shift focus from overwhelm to problem-solving.
- **Example:** "Production is 20% behind target—let's focus on the three bottlenecks."

4. Uplift with Vision

- Paint a *motivating picture of the future.*
- **Action:** Frame adversity as an opportunity for collective growth.
- **Example:** "We can be the team that performs best and leads the industry".

5. Set the Steps

- *Break down* the vision into actionable steps.
- **Action:** Set clear milestones and assign responsibilities.
- **Example:** "By next Friday, we'll have tested a new workflow to increase efficiency".

6. Unite Their Hearts

- Anchor progress in *shared values*.
- **Action:** Reinforce the emotional commitment to a greater purpose.
- **Example:** "We're not just hitting targets; we're building a culture of excellence."

7. Press for Action

- Drive *momentum with an immediate call to action*.
- **Action:** Set short-term challenges that drive engagement.
- **Example:** "Today, I challenge each of you to identify one area for improvement."

CONCLUSION
OWNING YOUR OUTER GAME

Leadership today is a test of resilience in the face of complexity—not a test of technical competence. The old playbooks—rigid hierarchies, top-down directives, and one-size-fits-all strategies—are crumbling under the weight of an increasingly volatile, uncertain and ambiguous world. Leaders who attempt to control every outcome, eliminate uncertainty, or impose stability through force soon find themselves in a paradox: the harder they try to stabilise, the more fragile their teams become.

This volume has explored the 'outer' dimension of neuro-resilient leadership. Yet, at its heart lies a fundamental truth: mastering one's own instinctual responses—the *Inner Game of Leadership*—is a prerequisite to leading collective intelligence—the *Outer Game of Leadership*. The leader's first responsibility is not to the organisation or the strategy, but to the governance of their own nervous system. A leader who cannot regulate their internal state will, consciously or not, impose their dysregulation onto others. The difference between a leader who fosters psychological safety and one who erodes it is often measured in moments: a misplaced sigh, a glance of disapproval, an impatient dismissal of an idea. These micro-signals are not trivial; they are the signals that shape the group's sense of safety, engagement and trust.

A leader does not sculpt results—they sculpt the conditions in which results emerge. The best leaders act as architects, designing an environment where intelligence, trust, and resilience become the natural state of the team.

Just as a skilled gardener does not *force* plants to grow but ensures they have the right soil, light, and water, the leader's craft is in shaping an environment where high performance becomes a natural consequence. And this is where the *Hive Mind* emerges—not as a mystical or abstract concept, but as the unseen force that dictates how teams function.

A well-led team is more than the sum of its individual members; it becomes an intelligent, self-regulating system. In the presence of safety, teams adapt fluidly, challenge ideas constructively, and move towards solutions with shared ownership. In its absence, even the most talented individuals retreat into defensive postures—rigidity, avoidance, and passive compliance. Talent, experience, and intelligence are wasted when people operate in self-protection mode. The determining factor between a team that thrives and one that suffocates is not raw ability but the level of psychological safety that exists between them.

Of course, some argue that psychological safety is a luxury, that too much comfort breeds complacency. But this is a fundamental misunderstanding. Safety is not the absence of challenge—it is the precondition for taking risks. The best teams are not those free from tension, but those where people trust that challenge will be met with curiosity rather than punishment.

Neuroscience affirms this: the human nervous system is constantly scanning for social cues of trust or threat. Stephen Porges' *Polyvagal*

Theory explains that when people feel psychologically unsafe, their physiology shifts into a defensive state, impairing cognitive flexibility, creativity and problem-solving. In contrast, safety unlocks engagement. A leader who understands this does not merely manage behaviour; they shape the very conditions under which performance becomes possible.

This is why neuro-resilient leadership is fundamentally a practice, not a position. The best leaders do not simply manage teams; they sculpt the environment in which high-functioning teams can emerge. They do this by developing three essential skills:

- First, they *regulate themselves under pressure*. A leader's state is the baseline for the team's state. Just as a fire crew does not look to a manual in a crisis but to the calmest, most experienced firefighter in the room, teams attune to their leader's nervous system. A leader who exudes control, confidence, and trust will set a physiological tone that allows others to follow suit.
- Second, they *understand and influence the Hive Mind*. Teams are not collections of individuals; they are interdependent, emergent systems. A leader who grasps this recognises that minor shifts in team culture—who gets to speak, how failure is handled, whether people feel truly heard—have profound effects on overall performance.
- Third, they *embed psychological safety into the team's fabric*. This is not a matter of policies or mission statements. It is a lived experience that must be reinforced in the moment-to-moment interactions that define group culture. Safety is not built in grand gestures but in subtle, repeated confirmations that it is safe to contribute, to challenge, to innovate.

And so, we return to two final questions:

Are you shaping the conditions where your team can operate at its highest level of intelligence, trust and resilience?

Or are you, however unintentionally, creating an environment where safety is uncertain, engagement is selective, and potential is left untapped?

Because in the end, leadership is not about the individual leader. It is about what they enable in others.

Power & Peril of Crowds

The most persistent illusion in leadership is the belief that teams are merely collections of individuals, each acting independently, making rational decisions based on self-interest. But human systems do not operate this way.

Teams are not like neatly arranged puzzle pieces, each contributing its part in isolation. They behave more like a murmuration of starlings —fluid, synchronised, shifting dynamically in response to unseen forces. Every action, hesitation and unspoken cue ripples through the group, shaping the collective behaviour. This is the Hive Mind—an emergent intelligence that can be greater than the sum of its parts or, just as easily, a breeding ground for dysfunction.

A well-led Hive Mind is a force multiplier, capable of processing complexity in real-time, integrating multiple perspectives and generating insights that no individual could reach alone. But when mismanaged, it collapses into rigidity, conformity and self-protection. Leaders who fail to understand this dynamic often misdiagnose the symptoms.

- Low engagement? *They assume a motivation problem.*
- Resistance to change? *A competence issue.*

- Lack of innovation? *A skills gap.*

Yet, the issue is rarely with individuals. It lies within the system itself.

The Silent Architecture

Every group develops an invisible architecture—an unspoken social contract dictating whose voice carries weight, whose ideas gain traction, and whose contributions fade into silence. This architecture is not crafted through formal policies or hierarchical structures but emerges through an intricate exchange of neurobiological signals.

In any team, there are those who speak freely and those who hesitate. Some people are interrupted mid-sentence while others command uninterrupted attention. Certain ideas spark discussion, while others sink beneath the surface, unacknowledged. Some emotions are mirrored and amplified, while others are met with blank stares. Risks are selectively rewarded or subtly punished.

Over time, these micro-patterns accumulate, forming the unwritten rules that govern group behaviour. Whether they foster psychological safety or corrode it depends largely on the leader, who—knowingly or not—is the chief architect of this invisible structure.

Intelligence vs Dysfunction

A team operating under psychological safety functions as adaptive intelligence—a collective network capable of learning, integrating new ideas, and navigating uncertainty with agility. But when safety is compromised, even subtly, this network does not simply slow down; it shifts from intelligence to defensiveness. The change is profound and immediate:

- *Silence becomes the safest strategy.* Instead of contributing insights, individuals hesitate, scanning for signs that speaking up is worth the risk.

- *Compliance replaces commitment.* People follow instructions, but without psychological investment. They execute, but they do not engage.
- *Innovation disappears.* Taking risks requires trust, and trust cannot exist in an environment where failure, ridicule, or exclusion loom as possibilities.

These are not abstract effects. Studies show that teams with low psychological safety experience heightened stress, slower problem-solving, and increased errors. Conversely, organisations that prioritise psychological safety report greater innovation, stronger cohesion, and resilience under pressure. Yet, the critical point is this:

Safety is not a logical conclusion—it is a **BIOLOGICAL STATE.**

Long before a person consciously decides to trust, engage, or contribute, their nervous system has already made the decision for them. This process (neuroception) operates below conscious awareness, continuously scanning the environment for signals of safety or threat.

- A hesitant glance from a leader can be interpreted as doubt.
- A tense posture can be processed as disapproval.
- An unexpected interruption can trigger a micro-threat response, shutting down creative thinking.

The leader's role, therefore, is not simply to declare a space safe, but to *demonstrate* it—through every interaction, every gesture and every moment of presence.

The Hive Mind's Regulator

At any given moment, a team is leaning toward one of two states:

1. *Adaptive Intelligence*—where psychological safety enables engagement, curiosity, and collective problem-solving.
2. *Defensive Rigidity*—where uncertainty and fear lead to withdrawal, compliance, and self-protection.

The leader sets the tone. Their ability to regulate their own state—to remain calm, clear, and composed under pressure—determines whether the Hive Mind becomes an asset or a liability. The question, then, is not whether you are leading a team. It is whether you are leading a Hive Mind that is awake, engaged, and adaptive—or one that is stagnant, hesitant, and defensive. Because in leadership, the difference is never neutral.

The Hidden Engine of High-Performance

The greatest misconception about psychological safety is that it is about being nice. It is not. It is not about eliminating conflict. It is not about ensuring people always feel comfortable. If anything, the opposite is true—psychologically safe teams argue more, not less. The difference? Their arguments are constructive rather than corrosive.

To understand psychological safety, envisage an orchestra. In an ideal performance, musicians challenge each other, adjust their timing, experiment with new phrasing, and lean into tension rather than avoiding it. If a conductor silences every error with a sharp look or a dismissive wave, the musicians learn one thing: play it safe. Stick to the notes. Take no risks. And while the music may remain technically accurate, it will lack something vital—*life*. The same is true in teams. The moment people fear that mistakes will be punished, creativity dies, and all that remains is compliance.

At its core, psychological safety is about *permission*—the permission to speak, to challenge, to contribute, to fail. It is what allows a team to think, adapt and problem-solve at its highest level of intelligence. Without it, even the most talented individuals will operate at a fraction of their capacity, diverting energy into self-protection rather than innovation, playing to authority rather than pursuing solutions.

But psychological safety is not something that can be declared. It must be *demonstrated*. A leader who says, 'We have an open-door policy' but subtly flinches when challenged has already communicated the *real rule*. And the nervous system, exquisitely attuned to signals of approval and rejection, does not negotiate with words—it obeys experience.

The Dual Nature of Psychological Safety

Psychological safety is not built in grand pronouncements or policy documents; it is forged in two complementary ways—*structural safeguards* that ensure safety exists beyond the leader's personal disposition, and *moment-to-moment priming* that determines whether safety is genuinely felt.

If psychological safety were a bridge, its *structural integrity* would be upheld by well-designed rules, routines and expectations. Without these, safety is fickle—dependent on personalities, shifting moods and external conditions.

Consider a Formula 1 pit crew. Every team member must act with precision under extreme time pressure, but they also know that mistakes will happen. If the culture treats errors as personal failings rather than process flaws, the crew will tighten up, hesitate, and play defensively. If, instead, errors trigger an immediate process review—'What do we adjust? What do we learn?'—then performance continuously improves.

High-performing teams operate in the same way. They establish clear norms and shared expectations—defining what engagement looks like, what risks are acceptable, and how failures are handled. They normalise structured reflection, using After-Action Reviews and debriefs to ensure that setbacks are treated as data, not as evidence of incompetence. They incorporate deliberate trust-building rituals, from check-ins to open forums, ensuring that vulnerability is met with reinforcement rather than silence. And they maintain transparency in decision-making, allowing people to see how their input shapes outcomes—because nothing erodes safety faster than the sense that engagement is merely performative.

But structures alone do not create safety. They create *predictability*. The human brain does not process 'safe' in the abstract—it determines safety in real-time interactions.

The Internal Reinforcement

Consider a leader who praises creativity but stiffens slightly when someone challenges their idea. A manager who invites feedback but habitually interrupts before an idea is fully formed. A team member who takes a risk, only to be met with an awkward silence rather than reinforcement. These micro-moments may seem trivial, but they accumulate. And in an environment where psychological safety is fragile, they signal: *'Think twice before speaking'*.

A leader who *masters* safety priming ensures that *safety is felt, not just stated*. This happens through:

- *Non-Verbal Acuity*: Safety is detected before it is understood. A leader who maintains a relaxed posture, uses open gestures, and sustains steady vocal prosody communicates receptivity. Conversely, a leader who glances at their phone mid-conversation signals disengagement, undermining any verbal assurances of openness.

- *Conversational Framing*: People rarely take risks in a vacuum. They take risks when the environment *invites* them to do so. Compare: 'Any thoughts?' versus 'I'm particularly interested in challenges to this idea—where might I be wrong?' The latter signals that dissent is not merely tolerated; it is *expected.*
- *Pacing & Leading*: Safety is not about dismissing tension—it is about meeting people where they are and guiding them forward. A hesitant team will not respond to forced enthusiasm, but they will follow a leader who first mirrors their state and then gradually shifts them towards engagement.
- *Co-Regulating Humour*: Well-placed humour acts as a neurological reset, shifting teams from defensiveness to receptivity. But *precision matters*—a joke at someone else's expense reinforces insecurity rather than trust.
- *Modelling Psychological Safety*: If a leader never admits uncertainty, their team will never feel safe to do so. If a leader never asks for help, their team will fear appearing incompetent. Safety is demonstrated, not demanded.

The Invisible Erosion

Leaders rarely *intend* to undermine safety—but they do so nonetheless, often in imperceptible ways. A team member voices a concern, and the leader unconsciously tenses their jaw. Someone suggests an unconventional approach, and the leader acknowledges it but swiftly moves on. No words were spoken, yet the lesson was learned: *risk is unwelcome here.*

Sometimes the erosion is more obvious. A leader claims to value openness but dominates discussions. They invite feedback but only act on suggestions that confirm their existing views. This inconsistency creates *uncertainty, and uncertainty is processed as a threat.*

Even well-intended corrections can become micro-punishments. A leader publicly corrects someone's comment rather than asking for clarification privately. A joke lands at a team member's expense, triggering laughter—except for the one who will think twice before speaking next time. None of these moments may seem dramatic, but the nervous system registers them all the same.

The Key to Collective Intelligence

Teams are not intelligent or unintelligent. They are either safe enough to engage fully or uncertain enough to withdraw.

A safe team will:

- Challenge outdated assumptions without hesitation.
- Think in solutions rather than self-protection.
- Generate creativity and insight that would not exist in a less safe environment.

An unsafe team will:

- Default to risk-avoidance and compliance.
- Suppress real concerns until they explode into conflict.
- Lose their ability to innovate under pressure.

Psychological safety is *not a soft concept*—it is the single greatest predictor of whether a team will function at adaptive intelligence or defensive paralysis.

And so the leader's responsibility is clear:

- Are you creating a climate where people can engage at their highest level of intelligence?
- Or are you unknowingly fostering an environment where silence and self-protection are the safest options?

Because leadership is never neutral. It always shapes the group—towards resilience or rigidity, towards engagement or withdrawal, towards intelligence or survival mode. Which will you choose?

Micro-Skills for Macro-Impacts

True leadership is not about grand gestures. It is not about rousing speeches, imposing authority, or the illusion of unwavering confidence. These may create moments of impact, but they do not sustain trust. Instead, true leadership rests on a far subtler foundation: the micro-skills that shape perception, behaviour, and engagement in real time.

A leader's influence does not come from declarations—it comes from signals. The most powerful shifts in psychological safety, engagement, and performance do not occur during formal leadership moments but in the quiet, imperceptible ones. The moments that accumulate into the team's lived experience.

This is why *The Elusive Obvious*—the subtle, easily overlooked signals—separates a high-trust, high-engagement team from one that operates in cautious self-protection.

The Currency of Leadership

A leader's words are never the full story. The team listens not just to what is said, but to how it is said, when it is said, and, most crucially, what remains unsaid.

A conversation is never just about content. A leader might nod imperceptibly, encouraging someone to continue—or glance at their phone mid-discussion, subtly signalling disinterest. They might pause for a breath after a team member speaks, inviting further thought—or jump in too quickly, shutting down exploration. These micro-signals operate beneath conscious awareness, but the brain processes them *before* logic, before reasoning, before words even register.

A leader might *say* that a team is safe to speak freely, but if their tone, posture, or facial expressions betray tension, the nervous system believes the signals, not the statement.

The best leaders refine this non-verbal acuity. They develop an invisible power—the ability to shape the emotional and psychological state of a room without uttering a single word.

What Sets Leaders Apart?

The leadership ideal is often thought of as charisma or authority. But the most effective leaders rely on precision in their micro-skills.

How a leader frames a question, a challenge, or a response determines whether it expands possibility or shuts it down. Consider two responses to the same situation:

- *"I don't think that will work—what else do you have?"*
- *"There's an interesting tension here—what assumptions are we making that might need adjusting?"*

One response narrows the map, making the speaker defensive. The other opens the map, inviting exploration. The difference is subtle, yet profound.

Most leaders underestimate the power of silence. The instinct is to fill gaps, keep conversations moving, respond quickly. But silence, when used deliberately, does something remarkable—it shifts ownership.

A leader who allows three seconds of silence after a team member speaks does not just create space. They signal *thoughtfulness*, they allow psychological safety to expand into the room, they invite reflection. The team, in turn, does not just wait for orders—they engage in thinking, discovery and ownership.

Trust is rarely built in grand moments. It emerges from a thousand micro-moments of reinforcement.

A slight nod as someone shares an idea signals 'keep going'. A pause before responding shows that their words are worth considering. A genuine 'That's an interesting perspective—I hadn't thought of that' encourages contribution without needing to declare agreement.

These moments seem insignificant, yet they determine whether a team expands into engagement or contracts into self-protection.

Leading with an Emotional Anchor

A leader's emotional state is contagious. If they radiate calm, clarity, and confidence, the team absorbs it. If they carry tension, anxiety, or frustration, the team mirrors that instead.

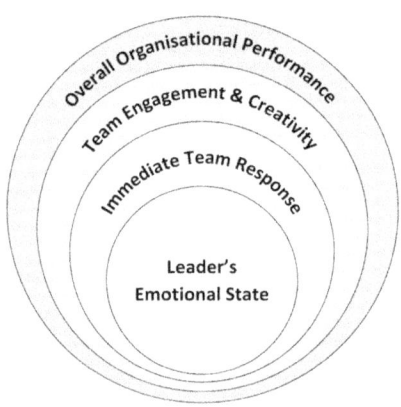

The Emotional Echo

This is co-regulation: the unseen mechanism behind psychological safety. Some leaders enter a room and immediately settle an anxious team; others inadvertently escalate tension without realising it.

The best leaders regulate themselves first:

- They take a breath before responding, steadying their nervous system before influencing others.
- They use warmth in their voice—tension in tone signals threat.
- They hold open, receptive body language—crossed arms or tense shoulders send defensive signals.

They are not reactive. They are stabilisers.

The Leader's Hidden Leverage

It is tempting to think of leadership as decisive action, bold vision, and strategic moves. And while these matter, they are meaningless without the micro-skills that shape team engagement.

A leader can *declare* psychological safety, but if their tone, posture, and micro-interactions contradict their words, their team will trust what they feel, not what they are told.

Micro-skills are not trivial. They are the architecture of trust. So, the question is not *what kind of leader you believe yourself to be*. A core question is:

What does your team's nervous system know to be true about you?

Storytelling for Safety & Trust

Leadership is not merely the art of giving direction—it is the art of shaping meaning. When uncertainty rises, when pressure mounts, when teams face setbacks, a leader's job extends far beyond managing tasks. It is about framing experience in a way that preserves engagement, reinforces trust, and strengthens cohesion. And the most powerful instrument for shaping meaning? *Storytelling.*

A story does not merely transmit information; it encodes safety, solidifies trust, and anchors a team to a shared reality. In the absence of a compelling narrative, people construct their own—and more often than not, these are narratives of doubt, fear, and fragmentation. The most effective leaders understand that the story people tell themselves is the story that dictates their actions. Whoever frames the narrative controls how reality is perceived.

Consider a ship lost in a storm. If the captain describes the situation as hopeless, the crew panics, focus fractures, and paralysis sets in. If the captain, instead, recounts tales of sailors who triumphed over tempests, if they frame the storm as a test rather than a threat, a shift occurs. Fear gives way to resolve. The same storm, reframed, demands courage rather than despair. This is not mere rhetoric—it is *neurobiology in action.*

Stories Shape Nervous Systems

The human brain does not process raw data in the same way it absorbs stories. Facts and figures engage logic, but stories ignite the limbic system—the emotional core that governs trust, motivation, and belonging.

A spreadsheet of metrics does not inspire engagement. A directive to 'work harder' does not ignite commitment. But a well-crafted narrative *does*. It activates the brain's emotional circuitry, transforming passive listeners into engaged participants. This is why leaders who master storytelling build teams that are not just compliant, but committed.

Yet not all stories unify. Some divide. Some deepen distrust. The difference lies in *how* the story is framed.

Framing for Engagement & Unity

Great storytelling for leaders follows an unspoken rhythm, a psychological sequence that moves teams from hesitation to clarity, from doubt to determination. The most effective narratives do not simply relay events—they shape the emotional landscape of a team, guiding their collective response.

A well-structured story:

- *Begins with alignment*—grounding the audience in a shared experience.
- *Creates agency*—framing the challenge as something that can be acted upon rather than suffered passively.
- *Connects individual struggles to collective purpose*—reinforcing team identity.
- *Provides a new lens for interpreting setbacks*—embedding resilience and adaptability.

Without this structure, a story risks misfiring—triggering resistance rather than engagement, scepticism rather than trust.

Cohesion Under Pressure

The story of Easy Company in *Band of Brothers* is one of leadership under extreme adversity. Facing the brutal conditions of war, these men did not survive on strategy alone—they survived on meaning.

- Their leader framed hardship as part of a larger mission, ensuring that suffering did not feel meaningless.
- Micro-moments of storytelling reinforced their shared identity, preventing doubt from fracturing their cohesion.
- Humour served as a resilience tool, shifting the emotional state of the group when pressure became overwhelming.

Elite military units, high-performance teams, and deeply bonded organisations all share this trait: a unifying narrative that transforms hardship into purpose. Without it, pressure drives fragmentation. The lesson?

> *A team's ability to persist through adversity is directly tied to the strength of their shared story.*

Reframing Hardship

In *Les Misérables*, Jean Valjean undergoes a transformation—not because his circumstances change, but because the *story he tells himself* does. At first, he sees himself as a victim of injustice, condemned to resentment. But through an act of trust and forgiveness, he rewrites his identity. He ceases to be the man to whom things *happen* and becomes the man who *chooses*.

This is the essence of effective leadership storytelling:

- It does not erase hardship—it reframes it in a way that restores agency.
- It does not ignore struggle—it contextualises struggle as a path to growth and impact.

A leader who does not provide this level of narrative clarity leaves their team adrift. And when uncertainty dominates, trust and motivation erode.

Everyday Leadership Storytelling

Storytelling in leadership is not an event—it is a habit. The best leaders use narrative not as a performance, but as a rhythm woven into daily interactions. A single well-told story can reframe a crisis, restore morale and deepen alignment.

Consider how the same situation can be framed differently:

- 'We failed to meet our target'.

- 'We discovered that our assumptions about X were incorrect—this insight now gives us a competitive advantage'.

- 'We don't know what will happen next'.
- 'Great teams are defined not by certainty, but by their ability to adapt. This is our moment to prove exactly that'.

- 'This is your role'.
- 'Let me tell you a story about how this role connects to something larger than the individual'.

A leader who does not actively shape the team's story leaves a vacuum—and a vacuum will always be filled, either by fear and doubt, or by purpose and resolve.

And so the fundamental question remains:

Are you crafting a story that strengthens your team's trust, resilience, and commitment? Or are you allowing uncertainty to write the story for you?

Because every team has a story. The only question is:

Who is telling it?

Neuro-Resilient Leader

Mastering leadership resilience is not about knowing—it is about doing. The most insightful frameworks, the most compelling theories, and the most well-reasoned strategies mean nothing if they are not woven into daily leadership practice.

A neuro-resilient leader does not merely memorise principles; they embody them. They create the conditions where trust, adaptability, and high performance emerge naturally, not as policies, but as lived realities.

Now comes the real challenge:

How do you ensure that neuro-resilience is not just a concept you appreciate, but a capability you develop and apply consistently?

The Art of Resilience

Leadership is not a fixed trait—it is a practice, much like the discipline of an athlete or the refinement of an artist. Every decision, every interaction, every reaction under pressure either strengthens or weakens the resilience of the leader and, by extension, their team.

Three pillars uphold neuro-resilient leadership:

- *Self-Regulation* – Mastering one's own nervous system before attempting to influence others.
- *Psychological Safety* – Ensuring trust is reinforced in every interaction.
- *Collective Intelligence* – Leading the Hive Mind rather than merely managing individuals.

These are not abstract ideals—they are disciplines, requiring continual refinement and a willingness to evolve.

The Leadership Anchor

A leader's emotional state is not private—it is public information, continuously broadcasted and absorbed by their team. If a leader is reactive, tense or defensive, the team unconsciously mirrors those states. If a leader is calm, clear, and grounded, the team regulates to that stability.

Think of a jazz musician improvising in a live performance. The ability to stay in flow—to absorb unpredictability without panic— determines the quality of the music. Leadership is the same. The ability to remain composed under pressure is not innate; it is cultivated.

To lead well under stress, a neuro-resilient leader must develop:

- *Situational Awareness of Their Own Nervous System*

Can you recognise the subtle shifts in your body before stress takes over? When pressure mounts, does your voice tighten, your breath shorten, or your movements become rigid? A leader who ignores these signals is already being led—by their own biology.

- *Deliberate Recovery Strategies*

A well-regulated leader builds rituals that prevent stress from accumulating. Deep breathing before a high-stakes meeting, structured reflection at the end of the day, or even the simple act of pausing before reacting—these micro-adjustments define the difference between a leader who steers the ship and one who is tossed by the waves.

If a leader cannot regulate themselves, they cannot regulate a team.

The Daily Test of Leadership

A team's engagement is not driven solely by motivation—it hinges on whether they feel safe enough to fully participate. Without psychological safety, ideas shrink, collaboration stalls, and decision-making narrows to defensive self-preservation.

See two meeting rooms. In one, team members hesitate before speaking, calculating whether their ideas will be dismissed or ridiculed. In the other, ideas flow freely, even the flawed ones, because people trust that failure will be treated as learning, not incompetence. The difference is not in the talent of the individuals—it is in the leadership that shapes the environment.

Psychological safety is built in two ways:

- *Through Structures that Enable Trust*

Are there clear norms for participation? Do feedback loops allow learning without fear of punishment? Are mistakes treated as useful data or as evidence of incompetence? If a team does not know the answer to these questions, their leader has already answered it for them—through neglect.

- *Through the Leader's Daily Behaviour*

How often do you interrupt rather than listen? Do your facial expressions match your words? When challenged, do you appear curious or defensive? Trust is not declared; it is demonstrated, in micro-moments, over time.

Psychological safety is not a policy—it is a lived experience, shaped by what leaders reinforce in every conversation.

From Compliance to Intelligence

Managing individuals is straightforward. Leading a collective intelligence is the real test. Consider a school of fish moving in synchrony. There is no single leader dictating each turn, yet the group moves with fluid precision, responding dynamically to threats and opportunities. A truly high-functioning team operates in the same way—not as a set of compliant individuals awaiting orders but as an intelligent, adaptive unit.

To cultivate this, a leader must ask:

- *Am I fostering an environment where people think freely, or are they filtering their ideas to fit my expectations?*

- *Do I encourage problem-solving, or am I the bottleneck for every decision?*
- *Is debate welcomed, or do people feel safer staying silent?*

High-performing teams exhibit:

- *Adaptive Intelligence* – They navigate complexity collectively, rather than defaulting to hierarchical decision-making.
- *Shared Ownership of Success and Failure* – Accountability is distributed, rather than concentrated in authority.
- *Active Challenge Without Fear* – A team that feels safe to question assumptions will always make better decisions than one that avoids conflict.

A neuro-resilient leader does not need to have all the answers. They need to create an environment where the best answers emerge. For a leader, the true test is not knowledge—it is embodiment. Consider this:

- When faced with stress, do you react instinctively or respond deliberately?
- Do your team members feel encouraged to challenge ideas, or do they tread carefully around leadership?
- When a problem arises, does your team collaborate dynamically, or do they wait for direction?

If these questions give you pause, that is not a failure—it is an invitation to the next level of leadership mastery.

Engaging Complexity

Leadership is shifting. Command-and-control models are crumbling under the weight of complexity. Static leadership styles collapse in environments that demand adaptability.

The leaders who will thrive in the coming decades are not those who dictate; they are those who understand and harness the human nervous system at scale.

Neuro-resilient leaders will be:

- The ones who create teams that adapt to rapid change rather than resist it.
- The ones who sustain high performance even in volatility.
- The ones who transform pressure into a strategic advantage rather than a source of dysfunction.

And so, the final challenge is not theoretical—it is deeply personal:

Are you ready to embody neuro-resilient leadership?

Because leadership is not about what you know—it is about what you reinforce in every interaction, every decision, and every moment you lead.

The Leadership Promise

So now, the question is not whether you *understand* these principles —it is whether you will *embody them*.

Neuro-resilient leadership is not about *occasional moments of inspiration*. It is about *consistent, deliberate practice*. Every conversation, every micro-interaction, every leadership decision is an opportunity to either:

- Reinforce *psychological safety* or *erode it*.
- Foster *adaptive intelligence* or *trigger self-protection*.
- Lead with *clarity and stability* or react from *uncertainty and stress*.

The world is not slowing down. Complexity is not easing. But leaders who master neuro-resilience will stand unshaken in the storm—guiding their teams through change, uncertainty and challenge with clarity, confidence, and precision.

Neuro-Resilient Imperative

Command-and-control leadership is not fading—it has already failed. The future will not belong to the most authoritative, but to the most adaptive. Not to those who impose certainty, but to those who cultivate resilience.

In a world of constant disruption, neuro-resilient leadership will be the defining edge between organisations that flourish and those that falter. Tomorrow's strongest leaders won't just be those with technical skill or authority. They will be those who:

- Regulate their own nervous system before attempting to influence others.
- Shape team conditions to drive performance through trust, not coercion.
- Frame challenges as narratives of resilience, ensuring uncertainty fuels engagement, not fear.

Organisations that fail to develop *neuro-resilient leadership* will struggle. They will experience:

- Increased *burnout and disengagement,* as employees operate in *states of chronic stress and uncertainty.*
- Higher *turnover and loss of talent,* as people seek environments where they feel *psychologically safe and valued.*
- Slower *adaptation to change,* as teams resist uncertainty rather than leaning into it with confidence.

Meanwhile, organisations that embed *neuro-resilience* into their leadership culture will *outperform, outlast, and outthink* their competition. The difference will not be in *IQ, strategy, or resources*—it will be in *how well leaders cultivate trust, engagement, and adaptability in the people they lead.*

Final Challenge

A leader does not sculpt results—they sculpt the conditions in which results emerge. The best leaders act as architects, designing an environment where intelligence, trust, and resilience become the natural state of the team. And so, one final challenge remains:

You are shaping the conditions of your team's future—right now, in real time. With every word, every pause, every glance. The question is not whether you are leading.

Are you leading them forward—or watching them retreat?

Because leadership is not about what you intend. It is about what your team feels, trusts, and dares to do under your influence. And every moment—whether you notice it or not—is tipping the balance. What will you choose?

AFTERWORD
THE LEADER YOU HAVE BECOME

There are few things more disheartening than watching a team unravel—not because of incompetence or ill will, but because something essential was missing. Not trust in the vision, but trust in the room. Not clarity of goals, but clarity of signals. And often, the leader watches this unfold helplessly, sensing the drift but unsure how to steady it. But you are not that leader. Not anymore.

By now, you've come to see that leadership doesn't begin when you speak—it begins when you enter: in the tone of your voice, the shape of your gaze, the rhythm of your breathing. Before any strategy is shared, before a single objective is declared, the group is already taking its cues—already forming its sense of *'safe'* or *'not yet'*.

And you've learned to lead there. In that invisible space. With precision, with calm, with purpose.

Perhaps you remember how things felt before: meetings where tension simmered under polite silence, conversations where ideas never quite landed, the subtle ways disengagement took root—not through revolt, but withdrawal. Not outright conflict, but a collective quiet that dulled every room you walked into.

But now? You read those cues early. You adjust. You soften your presence without losing authority. You create space not just for voices to speak, but for bodies to feel safe enough to contribute. You prime the room for honesty—not by demanding it, but by modelling it.

You've become the kind of leader who listens without interrupting the signal. Who notices the shift in energy before it becomes a fracture. Who understands that cohesion is not a motivational speech—it's a regulated field.

And when misalignment arises, as it always will, you don't resort to pressure. You reset the conditions. You return to the basics: co-regulation, pacing, alignment. You lead not through force, but through rhythm. Through clarity. Through deliberate signal and steady presence.

In the quiet hours of real leadership—the late-night email, the unexpected confrontation, the sudden shift in morale—this is the work that matters. This is what makes the difference between teams that crack and teams that hold.

You've practised techniques that aren't flashy, but they're foundational. You've implemented rituals that shape behaviour invisibly. You've built a container where trust doesn't have to be negotiated each day—it is simply assumed. And that's the mark of true psychological safety: when people no longer have to ask, *'Am I safe here?'*—because they just know.

But most of all, you've learned something deeper. That the outer game, for all its influence and signal work, still begins inside. That what you radiate is who you've become. That your presence is now a tool—one that calms, aligns, and strengthens others even in the midst of pressure.

The storm will still come. And when it does, your team will turn to you—not for all the answers, but for the atmosphere you create. For the clarity you bring. For the trust you carry into the room.

This isn't the end of your journey. It's the beginning of a new kind of leadership—one that leaves behind the old performance of control and steps into the quiet mastery of command.

You've become the emotional steward of the system. A conductor of invisible signals. A catalyst for shared resilience. Others will follow you now—not because they must, but because in your presence, they can breathe.

Paul O'Neill

November 2024

NOTES

INTRODUCTION

1. 'Nothingness is somethingness' is one of Keith McCullough's (CEO of Hedgeye) many memorable one-liners, which I have have used promiscuously, in many contexts.

1. THE HIVE MIND

1. Porges, S. W. (2011). *The Polyvagal Theory: Neurophysiological Foundations of Emotions, Attachment, Communication, and Self-Regulation*. Neuroception refers to the body's unconscious system for detecting safety, danger, or life threat.

2. SAFETY-EMBEDDED STRUCTURES

1. Whilst engagement's purpose was inspired by *Anecdote Circles*, the framing of the 'Appreciative Inquiry' is very much part of PACE Strengths DNA. In execution, the PACE Protocol structure and Meta Model are preeminent.

3. SAFETY PRIMING SKILLS

1. Bandler, R. (1985). *Using your brain—for a change: Neuro-linguistic programming*. Real People Press.
2. Extending co-regulation techniques to external stakeholders helps build trust, credibility, and rapport beyond the team setting.

PART ONE SUMMARY

1. Stephen Porges, Polyvagal Theory: Neurophysiological Foundations of Emotions, Attachment, Communication, and Self-Regulation.
2. The concept of 'Hive Mind' is used metaphorically to describe emergent intelligence in complex adaptive systems, similar to that observed in eusocial insects and flocking birds.
3. Neuroception is a term coined by Stephen Porges to describe the nervous system's unconscious detection of safety, danger, or life threat without cognitive awareness.
4. The 'Inner Game' refers to self-regulation; the 'Outer Game' involves group-level regulation and creating safety through behaviour, language, and presence.

5. AARs were developed by the U.S. Army to extract learning from events. The model fosters shared understanding without assigning blame.
6. 'Crumple & Toss' provides anonymity to reduce power distance and elicit more honest feedback, especially useful in hierarchical teams.
7. The PACE storytelling structure highlights Permission, Agency, Connection, and Embedding—used to shift emotional states and surface group wisdom.
8. Weak signals are early indicators of emerging issues or cultural dynamics. PACE Surfacing helps detect these through story-driven exploration.
9. Conscious breath regulation is a key co-regulation skill that allows leaders to influence collective nervous system states.
10. According to Polyvagal Theory, prosodic voice patterns signal safety to the vagus nerve, facilitating social engagement.
11. Mirroring metaphors and emotional intensity enhances empathy and psychological safety by demonstrating attunement.

INTRODUCTION

1. Paul Ekman's research on micro-expressions and universal emotional displays has shown how non-verbal cues trigger emotional judgments before verbal content is processed.
2. Joseph LeDoux and Antonio Damasio have demonstrated that emotional appraisal of threat and safety begins in subcortical structures before conscious awareness, reinforcing the evolutionary basis of non-verbal perception.
3. Daniel Goleman's model of emotional intelligence identifies self-awareness and self-regulation as foundational competencies for effective leadership and influence.
4. Chris Argyris and Donald Schön describe the gap between 'espoused theory' and 'theory-in-use,' suggesting leaders may unconsciously send signals that contradict their stated intentions.

PART TWO SUMMARY

1. Antonio Damasio's somatic marker hypothesis shows that physiological cues are processed before language, anchoring decisions in bodily experiences.
2. Albert Mehrabian's communication model suggests that trustworthiness is largely judged by non-verbal alignment between tone, expression, and content.
3. Bandler, R., & Grinder, J. (1975). *The Structure of Magic, Vol. 1*. Science and Behavior Books.
4. Bandler, R., & Grinder, J. (1979). *Frogs into Princes: Neuro Linguistic Programming*. Real People Press.
5. Grinder, M. (1993). *ENVoY: Your Personal Guide to Classroom Management*. Michael Grinder & Associates.
6. Bandler, R. (2008). *Get the Life You Want*. Health Communications; Grinder, M. (2003). *A Cat in the Doghouse*. Michael Grinder & Associates.
7. Grinder, M. (1993). *ENVoY: Your Personal Guide to Classroom Management*.

8. Grinder, M. (2004). *The Elusive Obvious: The Science of Nonverbal Communication*. Michael Grinder & Associates.
9. Grinder, M. (2004). *The Elusive Obvious: The Science of Nonverbal Communication*. Michael Grinder & Associates.
    Stephen Porges' Polyvagal Theory highlights how breathing patterns modulate vagal tone, which in turn influences how others perceive safety or threat in social interactions.
10. Bandler, R. (1993). *Time for a Change*. Neuro-Linguistic Programming Training Institute.
    NLP practices, as introduced by Richard Bandler, train perceptual flexibility through peripheral vision and subtle non-verbal pattern recognition, enhancing interpersonal calibration.
11. Grinder, M. (2005). *Charisma: The Art of Relationships*. Michael Grinder & Associates.
12. Synthesised concept based on the work of Michael Grinder, Paul Ekman & NLP observation of "clusters" – cf. Ekman, P. (2003). *Emotions Revealed*. Times Books.
    Virginia Satir's work on communication stances suggested that congruent body-language patterns influence relational impact and perception of authority.
13. Robert Dilts' behavioural modelling in NLP includes coordinated gesture-use to enhance linguistic anchoring and direct group attention during communication.
    See Grinder, M. (2004). *The Elusive Obvious*.
14. Grinder, M. (2004). *The Elusive Obvious*, esp. in police training & de-escalation chapters.
15. The 'Milton Model,' developed by Bandler and Grinder, includes embedded command structures and tonal shifts such as pauses and whispers to guide attention below the level of conscious resistance.
    Grinder, M. (2004). *The Elusive Obvious*.

INTRODUCTION

1. Ralph Stacey, *Complexity and Organizational Reality*, Routledge, 2001.
2. Dave Snowden, "The Cynefin Framework: Decision Making in Context," *Harvard Business Review*, 2007.
3. Stephen W. Porges, *The Polyvagal Theory: Neurophysiological Foundations of Emotions, Attachment, Communication, and Self-Regulation*, Norton, 2011.
4. https://www.richardbandler.com/
5. Paul D. MacLean, *The Triune Brain in Evolution*, Springer, 1990.

8. "BAND OF BROTHERS"

1. Dave Snowden, cited in "The Use of Narrative in Knowledge Management," *KM World*, 2000.
2. Based on a real merger case story (anonymised), where leadership narrative helped stabilise emotional uncertainty and define the new shared identity.

9. "LES MISÉRABLES"

1. Dave Snowden, "Narrative and Complex Systems," *Cognitive Edge Blog*, 2009.
2. Nelson Mandela, Rivonia Trial Speech, April 20, 1964.
3. Mahatma Gandhi, Speech during the Quit India Movement, August 8, 1942.
4. Abraham Lincoln, Gettysburg Address, November 19, 1863.
5. The 4Cs—Compassion, Credibility, Cognition, and Campaign—are adaptive leadership traits for narrative engagement developed by the author to accompany the FOCUS UP framework.
6. Composite leadership narrative drawn from multiple team transformation projects led by the author between 2018–2022.
7. The story of Jerry illustrates how psychological safety ruptures propagate through teams if left unresolved—an example of emotional contagion in social neuroscience
8. The Triune Brain model (Reptilian, Mammalian, Primate) was first developed by neuroscientist Paul MacLean and has since been applied in organisational and leadership studies
9.

PART THREE SUMMARY

1. See: Porges, S. (2011). *The Polyvagal Theory*; also Snowden, D. (2005). "Narrative as Sense-Making in Complex Systems." These works underpin the role of narrative in triggering safety responses

BIBLIOGRAPHY

Books

Bandler, R. (1985). *Using your brain for a change: Neuro-linguistic programming.* Real People Press.

Bandler, R. (2008). *Get the life you want: The secrets to quick and lasting life change with neuro-linguistic programming.* Health Communications.

Bandler, R., & Grinder, J. (1975). *The structure of magic I: A book about language and therapy.* Science and Behavior Books.

Bandler, R., & Grinder, J. (1979). *Frogs into princes: Neuro linguistic programming.* Real People Press.

Bandler, R., & LaValle, J. (1996). *Persuasion engineering.* Meta Publications.

Bion, W. R. (1961). *Experiences in groups: And other papers.* Tavistock Publications.

Brown, B. (2012). *Daring greatly: How the courage to be vulnerable transforms the way we live, love, parent, and lead.* Gotham Books.

Cuddy, A. J. C. (2015). *Presence: Bringing your boldest self to your biggest challenges.* Little, Brown and Company.

Damasio, A. R. (1994). *Descartes' error: Emotion, reason and the human brain.* Putnam.

Damasio, A. R. (1999). *The feeling of what happens: Body, emotion and the making of consciousness.* Heinemann.

Dana, D. (2018). *The polyvagal theory in therapy: Engaging the rhythm of regulation.* W. W. Norton.

Edmondson, A. C. (2018). *The fearless organisation: Creating psychological safety in the workplace for learning, innovation, and growth.* Wiley.

Goleman, D. (1995). *Emotional intelligence: Why it can matter more than IQ.* Bantam Books.

Goleman, D. (2006). *Social intelligence: The new science of human relationships.* Hutchinson.

Grinder, M. (1996). *ENVoY: Your personal guide to classroom management.* Michael Grinder & Associates.

Grinder, M. (2006). *A healthy classroom: Educational group dynamics.* Michael Grinder & Associates.

Grinder, M. (2009). *Charisma: The art of relationships.* Michael Grinder & Associates.

Jacobs, B. (2014). *The embodied leader: A somatic approach to developing your leadership.* Jossey-Bass.

Kahneman, D. (2011). *Thinking, fast and slow.* Farrar, Straus and Giroux.

Lakoff, G., & Johnson, M. (1980). *Metaphors we live by.* University of Chicago Press.

LeDoux, J. (1996). *The emotional brain: The mysterious underpinnings of emotional life.* Simon & Schuster.

Levine, P. A. (1997). *Waking the tiger: Healing trauma*. North Atlantic Books.

MacLean, P. D. (1990). *The triune brain in evolution: Role in paleocerebral functions*. Springer.

Mandela, N. (1994). *Long walk to freedom: The autobiography of Nelson Mandela*. Little, Brown and Company.

Mandelbrot, B. B. (2004). *The (mis)behaviour of markets: A fractal view of financial turbulence*. Profile Books.

Porges, S. W. (2011). *The polyvagal theory: Neurophysiological foundations of emotions, attachment, communication, and self-regulation*. W. W. Norton.

Sinek, S. (2009). *Start with why: How great leaders inspire everyone to take action*. Penguin Books.

Snowden, D. J., & Boone, M. E. (2007). A leader's framework for decision making. *Harvard Business Review*, 85(11), 68–76.

Stacey, R. D. (2007). *Strategic management and organisational dynamics* (5th ed.). Pearson Education.

Sutton, R. I. (2007). *The no asshole rule: Building a civilised workplace and surviving one that isn't*. Business Plus.

van der Kolk, B. A. (2014). *The body keeps the score: Brain, mind and body in the healing of trauma*. Viking.

Wheatley, M. J. (2006). *Leadership and the new science: Discovering order in a chaotic world* (3rd ed.). Berrett-Koehler Publishers.

Zinsser, W. (2006). *On writing well: The classic guide to writing nonfiction* (30th anniversary ed.). Harper Perennial.

Audio/CD Recordings

Bandler, R. (2000). *Soften Too!* [Audio CD]. Excellence Quest Training International.

Bandler, R. (2011). *Persuasion Engineering* [CD set]. NLP Life Training.

Video/DVD Recordings

Bandler, R. (1993). Anxiety relief and phobia cure [Video]. NLP Seminars Group International.

Bandler, R. (1994). Personal enhancement series [DVD series]. NLP Comprehensive.

Bandler, R. (2002). Trance-formations live [DVD]. NLP Life Training.

Bandler, R. (2004). Richard Bandler in Konstanz: Advanced NLP Seminar [DVD]. NLP Life Training / NLP Seminars Group International.

ACKNOWLEDGMENTS

I would also like to acknowledge **Richard Bandler**—not only for his groundbreaking contributions to NLP, but for the ripple effect his work continues to have on those of us helping others navigate change. I have applied his people-change technologies for over twenty-five years, ever emboldened by supportive discoveries in neuroscience. And though the PACE framework took shape in a different context, it carries his unmistakable DNA: precision, playfulness, and the deep belief that change can be fast, embodied, and lasting.

A quiet but foundational thanks to **Michael Grinder**. His work in non-verbal communication, presence, and group influence did more than inform the micro-skills in Part Two—it sharpened them. Long before the terms *psychological safety* or *co-regulation* gained traction in boardrooms, Michael was modelling them with chalk, pause, and presence. This book builds on the architecture he laid down—an architecture of breath, gaze, and grounded attention.

My sincere thanks to **Francinne Kaye Gacilo**, whose sharp eye and creative mind brought this book to life in more ways than one. As a digital media specialist with a flair for graphic design, Francinne not only proofread the manuscript with care but also contributed a series of interior graphics that added clarity, elegance, and visual depth to the pages. Her work helped turn concepts into compelling visuals—and for that, I'm deeply grateful.

ABOUT THE AUTHOR

Paul O'Neill is trusted by professionals in business, heavy industry, medical and mental health, and elite sports as consultant, coach and guide. For more than twenty-five years, he's been doing exactly that: guiding individuals, teams and entire organisations through the thickets of change, chaos and contradiction with a calm intensity that refuses to settle for surface solutions.

His leadership record spans continents and industries, yet his work never follows a formula. That's the point. Real transformation, he insists, can't be imposed or standardised. It must be built, brick by deliberate brick, in the language, rhythm, and logic of those who live it.

Clients across Australia, New Zealand, the UK, North America, and South Africa describe him as 'visionary', 'invaluable', 'a lifelong friend' - though the word most often repeated is 'transformational'. Not because Paul performs miracles, but because he hands the tools over. He trains people to recognise patterns, to respond to pressure with composure, to build resilience that sticks - not just in the individual nervous system, but in the culture of entire teams.

Paul's training and coaching in neuro-resilience skills, verbal and non-verbal skills, group dynamics, complex problem-solving, stakeholder engagement and adaptive strategic leadership has helped professionals across sectors rewrite their stories - by both negating the harsh effect change can have on the leaders, as well as by navigating their group through it differently. He's known for making the complex understandable, for challenging the status quo with warmth and rigour, and for turning the work of change into something deeply human and fiercely practical.

He remains, above all else, a practitioner. Someone who steps in, shoulder to shoulder, as a guide; and he stays until the work is done.

If you've reached the edge of what you know and understand, Paul is someone you want in the room.

www.ingramcontent.com/pod-product-compliance
Lightning Source LLC
Chambersburg PA
CBHW061725070526
44583CB00024B/3015